WHERE STRANGE GODS CALL

Harry Hervey was born in November 1900 in Beaumont, Texas. In 1923 he got a job as a cruise director travelling through Asia, and this gave him the opportunity to explore a number of countries and cities. The resultant book, *Where Strange Gods Call*, was called 'extraordinary' by the *Chicago Tribune*. Today Hervey is best remembered for his screenplays, including *Shanghai Express* which was released in 1932.

Paul French, who has introduced and annotated this reprint, was born in London and lived and worked in Shanghai for many years. His book *Midnight in Peking* was a *New York Times* bestseller and a BBC Radio 4 Book of the Week.

Also by Paul French:

Destination Peking

Strangers on the Praia

Destination Shanghai

City of Devils: A Shanghai Noir

Midnight in Peking: How the Murder of a Young Englishwoman Haunted the Last Days of Old Peking

The Badlands: Decadent Playground of Old Peking

Bloody Saturday: Shanghai's Darkest Day

Supreme Leader: The Making of Kim Jong-un

Betrayal in Paris: How the Treaty of Versailles Led to China's Long Revolution

The Old Shanghai A-Z

Through the Looking Glass: China's Foreign Journalists from Opium Wars to Mao

Carl Crow – A Tough Old China Hand: The Life, Times, and Adventures of an American in Shanghai

North Korea Paranoid Peninsula – A Modern History

Where Strange Gods Call

Harry Hervey's 1920s Hong Kong, Macao and Canton Sojourns

By Harry Hervey
(1924)

Annotated by Paul French

BLACKSMITH BOOKS

China Revisited: No. 1 of a series

Where Strange Gods Call

ISBN 978-988-75547-5-2

Published by Blacksmith Books
Unit 26, 19/F, Block B, Wah Lok Industrial Centre,
37-41 Shan Mei Street, Fo Tan, Hong Kong
Tel: (+852) 2877 7899
www.blacksmithbooks.com

Illustrations by Christopher Murphy Jr.

Cover photo: Buddhist monks playing Weiqi (the game of
Go), Temple of the Five Hundred Gods (華林寺), Guangzhou.
Photograph by John Thomson. Image courtesy of Special
Collections, University of Bristol Library (www.hpcbristol.net).
Many thanks to Jamie Carstairs and Robert Bickers of the
Historical Photographs of China project at the University
of Bristol.

CONTENTS

ABOUT CHINA REVISITED

China Revisited is a series of extracted reprints of mid-nineteenth to early-twentieth century Western impressions of Hong Kong, Macao and China. The series comprises excerpts from travelogues or memoirs written by missionaries, diplomats, military personnel, journalists, tourists and temporary sojourners. They came to China from Europe or the United States, some to work or to serve the interests of their country, others out of curiosity. Each excerpt is fully annotated to best provide relevant explications of Hong Kong, Macao and China at the time, to illuminate encounters with historically interesting characters or notable events.

Given the prejudices of the era, what are we to take from these works? Some have a stated agenda, namely colonial control and administration of Hong Kong and Macao, or else proselytising and saving souls for the Christian religion. This is generally obvious in the writing. Others have no stated objective but impressions of the regions, their peoples, and cultures are products of their time and value systems. There is an unsurprising tendency to exoticize, make generally unfavourable comparisons to their home cultures and societies, and to misunderstand what they are witnessing.

They are – whether from American or European sources – invariably from men and women of some formal education. Their acquaintances are among the colonial authorities and foreign diplomats. These "filters" mean that invariably we are given an elite view of China; this is not the experience of the non-officer class sailor, merchant seaman, regular soldier, or working-class visitor. Even before we get to racial prejudice we are encountering class prejudice.

The writers in this series were all men and women of their time, encountering China at specific times in its history. Most of them were visitors or residents for a limited amount of time. However, some, notably the missionaries, did remain for longer – decades in some cases. In general the only foreigners who had credible local language skills were the missionaries, or British colonial district officers and their Portuguese equivalents in Macao, along with some diplomat-scholars. Assumptions were made, prejudices voiced, yet all of these writings have something to reveal of the encounters from which they derived.

FOREWORD

"Pages Out of the East"

For a number of years I had been thinking about a way to resurrect the Asian memoirs, short stories and movie treatments of the American author, scriptwriter, journalist, traveller, aesthete and Asia-Hand, Harry Hervey. I realised this would begin to be possible when I read that, under the United States of America Copyright Term Extension Act of 2019, the majority of media from a previous year in the United States was to enter the public domain after the expiration of its copyright term. The year 2019 was also to be the first year in an annual process, where 1923 works had become public domain that year, then 1924 works would do so in 2020, and so on annually. The Copyright Term Extension Act therefore opens up a fantastic treasure trove of 1920s writing to consider reprinting. Including Harry Hervey…

Hervey's travelogue of his time in Hong Kong, Macao and Southern China includes his interview with Dr Sun Yat-sen. This is perhaps the last interview Dr Sun gave to an American writer before his death less than a year later. The travelogue was originally published in 1924 in the United States and in 1925 in Great Britain. The travelogue excerpts here reprinted and annotated form two chapters of his memoir of his 1923/1924 journey through East and South East Asia published as *Where Strange Gods Call: Pages Out of the East*. That book entered the public domain on January 1, 2020.

INTRODUCTION

Harry Hervey's Asian Sojourns

Harry Hervey, who is now probably best remembered for his later somewhat scandalous and salacious "Southern" novels, was a young man with a passion for all-things Asian.[1] He toured the wider East and South East Asian region at least twice in the 1920s, published several memoirs of those trips, as well as a number of

---

1 Most notably *The Damned Don't Cry* (New York: The Greystone Press, 1939). The *Kirkus* review upon publication noted, 'A flamboyant story of decadence in the old South – Savannah. The girl Zelda, was born in the gas-house district, of whores and drunks, but has herself an innate refinement that strives upward. She has her dreams – but a night of love and passion blasts her hopes, and she bears her child. The doors of hope reopen – again Fate intervenes, and she turns her back, marries for security and raises the child. The story is the story of her revenge on the city – and on the house of her dreams. Hervey is too facile, he never quite succeeds in being as hard-boiled as he pretends, and he goes in for some pretty purple writing, and some mystic-romanticism. Pretty cheap, though glossed over. A sure renter – but not for discriminating readers.'

novels set in Asia. Though the rest of his life was spent in the United States he was to constantly travel back to Asia in his short stories and movie scripts. Most famously in his original treatment for the film *Shanghai Express*, which was bought by Josef von Sternberg and eventually (with a script by Jules Furthman) became the Marlene Dietrich, Anna May Wong and Clive Brook movie of 1932.

However, Hervey isn't much remembered these days, if at all, for his Asian-themed works. One or two of his novels have been republished and, in 2017, Harlan Greene published the first biography of Hervey, *The Damned Don't Cry – They Just Disappear: The Life and Works of Harry Hervey*.[2] Greene's biography reclaims Hervey as a southern writer as well as a gay writer. To date it is by far the best biographical source we have on Hervey.[3] I am indebted to Greene and hope this small volume goes some way to further restoring Hervey's reputation as an important American writer.

Hervey was a man of his time. This meant that his sexuality was only ever alluded to obliquely; references

2   Harlan Greene, *The Damned Don't Cry – They Just Disappear: The Life and Works of Harry Hervey* (Columbia, SC: University of South Carolina Press, 2017).

3   I would add my own essay of Hervey and the inspiration behind his treatment for *Shanghai Express*, 'Harry Hervey's Peking of the Imagination' contained in Paul French, *Destination Peking* (Hong Kong: Blacksmith Books, 2021).

merely note that he had "travelling companions", "close friends" etc as euphemisms. He was also sometimes a man of his period in terms of language. Hervey certainly likes to emphasise the exotic though, I would argue, he is consistently sympathetic to Asia and Asian people, critical at times of colonial and imperial attitudes, and highly supportive of China's 1911 republican revolution (*Xinhai*). However, he does use some terms that are now not generally used and rightly frowned upon – 'Chinaman' particularly. Hervey's usage should be framed and contextualised. The term was widely used in the nineteenth century both as a pejorative and more than usually with generally derogatory overtones. I would argue that set against Hervey's body of writing on Hong Kong, Macao and Southern China (i.e. the passages reprinted here), Hervey's use of the term in 1924 is not intended as malicious.

Hervey in 1924 was on the cusp of a vigorous debate about to occur over the use of the term in the United States. In the 1930s American writers and "China Hands", such as Carl Crow, began to criticise people using the term "Chinaman". Crow, and others – Sinologists, Chinese intellectuals in America and the Chinese Embassy in Washington – engaged with newspapers and authors using the term as well as entering into long correspondences with the compilers of the *Oxford English*

Dictionary concerning the term. The editors of the OED in England accepted the argument that 'Chinaman' had gone out of fashion and was now a derogatory term and therefore offensive in 1938. The OED said that they would consider revising their entry. Crow was encouraged enough to fire off letters to the compilers of other English language dictionaries in America encouraging them to alter their entries too.[4]

* * *

Harry Hervey was born in November 1900 in Beaumont, Texas. His parents were jobbing hotel managers moving regularly from establishment to establishment across the south and south west of the United States. Hervey attended local schools and then, in 1916, the Sewannee Military Academy in Tennessee for three years prior to a year at the Georgia Military Academy in Atlanta. After school Hervey worked briefly as a reporter on the *Atlanta Constitution* and as a clerk for the Texas Oil Company.

---

4   For those interested, Crow's correspondence on the use of the term "Chinaman" can be found in the Carl Van Doren Archive at Princeton University Library's Department of Rare Books and Special Collections. See Letter from Lowell Thomas to Carl Crow, 10 September 1941, Crow Archive, folder 187C. Also Letter from Carl Crow to Carl Van Doren, 4 April 1938 and Copy of Letter from Carl Crow to HW Fowler, Oxford University Press, 10 March 1938.

Initially he wrote after work and on weekends. His first novel was *Caravans By Night, A Romance of India*, published in 1922 by The Century Company in New York. The novel was generally well-received – Hervey was described as '…the most promising young romancer in the country' by one prominent critic, though the novel was all based on secondary research. He followed this up swiftly with a second novel, *The Black Parrot, A Tale of the Golden Chersonese*,[5] which ranges around Asia from Malaysia to Lhasa. The book was abridged and serialised in newspapers across America. The reviewer for the *St. Louis Globe-Democrat* waxed lyrically: "*The Black Parrot* is a dream of liveliness interrupted by a nightmare… I was delighted with the flow of words, the suggestiveness of the pictures, but most of all with the naïve sincerity of its fancifulness.'[6] But by the time the reviews appeared Hervey was already in Asia.

In 1923 Hervey used his parents travel industry connections to get a job as a cruise director travelling through Asia. How good he was as a cruise director is unrecorded, but he certainly seems to have found time

---

5   Harry Hervey, *The Black Parrot, A Tale of the Golden Chersonese* (New York: The Century Company, 1923).

6   WE Matthews, 'Mysterious East Vividly Portrayed in Hervey Novel', *St. Louis Globe-Democrat*, September 22, 1923, p.15.

to explore a number of countries and cities. The resultant book, published a year later, *Where Strange Gods Call*, was called 'extraordinary' by the *Chicago Tribune*, who provided potential readers with a good overview of the book:

"*Where Strange Gods Call*, by Harry Hervey, is something more than one of those green jacketed travel books. It is the spirited chronicle of a romantic young man who goes adventuring all over the east: across the Pacific to Zamboanga, in the Philippines, to Japan and China, through the Malay archipelago that Joseph Conrad wrote about, to India. This is really an extraordinary book in its color and imagery and romance. It is not merely a book of places, but of places and people… Mr. Hervey has put zest and charm into the characters that stray across the pages of *Where Strange Gods Call*…'[7]

The Los Angeles Times also praised the book and spoke to Hervey about his next trip to Asia, with an unnamed companion. 'We may be gone six months, or six years,' Hervey tells the paper. He wants to get to Angkor, the Cambodian jungles, Rangoon, the Shan States, the Himalayas, and finally Tibet. He'll write it all up and call it *Drums at Dusk*.'[8] The unnamed companion was

---

7   *Chicago Tribune*, October 5, 1924, p.51.

8   *The Los Angeles Times*, December 21, 1924, p.56. *Drums at Dusk* sadly never transpired though Hervey did write a later

the Charleston-born and based editor, author and actor, Carleton A Hildreth who was to remain Hervey's partner until Hervey's death in 1951.

Hervey, hired by *McCall's Magazine*, did make one last trip to Asia, specifically to French Indo-China (Vietnam and Cambodia) in 1925. He was accompanied by Hildreth again. Hervey wrote up this trip as *Travels in French Indo-China*, published in 1928.[9]

* * *

After returning from his third trip to Asia Hervey moved to Savannah, Georgia, and lived at the DeSoto Hotel with his mother and Carleton Hildreth (who was working as a proof-reader on the *Savannah Morning News*).[10] The couple did not stay long but, in 1926, moved to Charleston, South Carolina. Over the next years they summered in New York City and wintered in Charleston with occasional visits to Savannah to see Hervey's mother. It was a productive time – several novels and plays, invariably on "Eastern themes". The Indo-China trip produced two novels – *Congaï, Mistress of Indochine*

---

travelogue of the Indo-China region – see footnote 9.

9   Harry Hervey, *Travels in French Indo-China* (London: Thornton Butterworth, 1928).

10   The DeSoto Hotel in Savannah opened in 1890 on East Liberty Street. It remains in business today.

and *King Cobra: Mekong Adventures in French Indochina*, both published in 1928.[11] Additionally a play in 1927, which quickly became a Fred Niblo-directed silent movie with Clive Brook and Gilda Gray as Takla, *The Devil Dancer*. The movie, which received an Academy Award nomination for cinematography, is now sadly "lost" and no prints or negatives are known to have survived. Hervey also started writing about America – *Red Ending*, a 'Southern Gothic' novel published in 1929, rather shocked the more conservative elements of Charleston society with Hervey's portrayal of the town.[12]

Hervey was also doing well writing screenplays. He had some involvement in the title cards for the movie version of *The Devil Dancer*, and then was hired to write a script for Tallulah Bankhead, which became the 1931 movie, *The Cheat*.[13] Hervey and Hildreth moved to Hollywood for a time to work on the film. The movie is

11   Harry Hervey, *Congaï: Mistress of Indochine* (London: Thornton Butterworth, 1928); *King Cobra: Mekong Adventures in French Indochina* (New York: Cosmopolitan Book Corporation, 1928).

12   Harry Hervey, *Red Ending* (New York, H Liveright Inc., 1929).

13   For *The Devil Dancer* Hervey is officially credited with "story". Edwin Justus Mayer and Alice DG Miller are credited with the "title cards". For *The Cheat* Hervey is credited with the silent film script along with Hector Turnbull.

set in America, but there's quite a few Orientalist tropes – a lover who has been corrupted by "The Far East", while Bankhead (who considered the script 'banal') spends much of the movie in an elaborate Chinese dress of some Hollywood concoction. Hervey had more success with the treatment for *Shanghai Express*, which Josef von Sternberg bought. However Hervey had no involvement with the movie beyond successfully selling the thirty-three-page treatment to the director.[14]

Hervey's archive is held at the Georgia Historical Society in Savannah.[15] It contains several treatments submitted to various Hollywood studios with Asian themes including comedies set in Shanghai and melodramas set in China's interior, inter-war Peking, and a final one being set in Seoul on the opening day of the Korean War. These treatments were mostly rejected, or died early in development. However, Hervey was periodically hired by Hollywood to write several movie scripts, with the best known being the

---

14 Hervey's full treatment is contained in Folder 11, The Joseph Freeman Papers, Hoover Institution, Stanford University, California.

15 'The Carleton Hildreth and Harry Hervey Papers (MS1695)', Georgia Historical Society, Savannah, Georgia. My thanks to Megan Walsh Gerard in relation to finding these papers.

Bob Hope, Bing Crosby and Dorothy Lamour musical vehicle *Road to Singapore* (1940).[16]

Hervey continued to live in Charleston and Savannah with Carleton Hildreth, writing movie treatments and novels, which were often co-researched with and edited by Hildreth. He died in 1951 of throat cancer. Hildreth died in 1977. They are both buried in Savannah's Bonaventure Cemetery.

Harry Hervey, 1933

---

16   Hervey is credited with "original story"; Dan Hartman and Frank Butler for the screenplay.

WHERE STRANGE GODS CALL

(1)

(This text and spellings taken from *Where Strange Gods Call: Pages Out of the East, Chapters 10 & 11,* by Harry Hervey, London: Thornton Butterworth Ltd, first British edition, 1925)

IMPERIAL YELLOW

1

China.

Few are they who have not climbed the jade staircase of fancy to dreams spun by that word... ivory and cedarwood and silks, and tall junks cargoed with spices and women... The first time I saw its coast was in the early morning. The raw air of the north had been healed by soft tropical winds. To the landward a reflected hazy light smouldered on the sea, stretching, like a golden atrium, to the hills that bosomed the shore. Bare, sombre hills, and brown as rust; the hills of Han. That they were part of China, a place so intimate in my fancy, seemed incredible, a thrilling mirage, result of the warm, heady sunlight that I drank in so fiercely. China! Ivory and cedar-wood and silks... A sweet delirium stole into me. I yearned for extravagant adventure – a role in revolutionary intrigue or some equally preposterous hazard.

This pleasant madness lingered through the morning; and when the ship swung into the roadstead of Hong-kong it was fed with new exhilaration. [17] The harbour lay like a brilliant green arena in an amphitheatre of encircling mountains; a watery stage where ships of the world, every manner of craft from armoured cruisers to Chinese boats with bat-wing sails, were gathered in superb display. We docked at Kowloon, on the mainland; and across the way, moated by a narrow channel, rose the city of Hong-kong, the myriad buildings along the Bund[18] deploying their

---

17   Spellings of Hong Kong as alternatively Hong-kong and Hongkong were common up until the early 1950s.

18   *Hobson-Jobson* defines Bund as 'any artificial embankment, a dam, dyke, or causeway.' The word is from Persian via Urdu. However, strictly speaking Hervey uses the term wrongly here. *Hobson-Jobson* tells us that Bund 'is naturalized in the Anglo-Chinese ports. It is there applied especially to the embanked quay along the shore of the settlements. In Hong Kong alone

tiers of houses as the town swept upward on a surge of green. Hanging over the city, like a great naked emotion towering above the artificiality of human existence, was the Peak, the highest of the band of mountains that coronals Victoria Island.[19] It was thrilling, that vista; and it put a new whip and rhythm into my blood. Indeed, of all the ports that burn in my memory – harbours poignantly quiet, roadsteads active with shipping, bays of the tropics and of a colder hemisphere – none are as magnificent as Hong-kong.

As the ship warped in at the Kowloon docks, sampans drifted alongside, manoeuvred by sexless-looking creatures whose shrill, attenuated voices proclaimed them women. In some of the boats were bamboo cages overcrowded with squawking birds, yellow-crested cockatoos, and grey and pink parrots. It was a charming scene until I perceived

---

this is called (not *bund*, but) *praia* (Portuguese for 'shore'), probably adopted from Macao.' This is indeed so and the term *praia* was widely used until the later twentieth century when 'shore' or 'harbour front' were most commonly used. I can find no other references to the harbour front at Hong Kong as a bund though, of course, the term was common in the treaty ports of China and remains in common usage when referred to the Huangpu River waterfront in Shanghai. Henry Yule & AC Burnell, *Hobson-Jobson: The Definitive Glossary of British India – A Selected Edition* (Ed. Kate Teltscher), (Oxford: Oxford University Press, 2013).

19   i.e. Hong Kong Island.

that the sampan women were there for a twofold purpose to salvage the swill emptied from the ship as well as to market their feathery merchandise...

The dock was a place of clamour and chaos; shrill voices of the coolies, the rattle of man-propelled trucks and carts; naked yellow backs, flying legs, and swift hands that worked the tie-lines and mooring-ropes. I sifted through this noisy sphere to the ferry-boat; glided across the channel to Hong-kong.

Spacious esplanades bordered the water-front, and wide streets ran between stone buildings and narrow arcades – roads throbbing with an amazing traffic that seemed to have drawn into its pulse all the colours of the East and West. Dark men from Coromandel and Ceylon.[20] Bronzed men from Bombay. Yellow men from the interior provinces where sun and wind burnish the skin. Ivory men from the cities and coast towns. Pallid men from lands untouched by Oriental seas... Tall Sikh policemen stood at the intersection of streets, no less proud than the white men who strode by with an air of conscious superiority; rickshaws raced past carrying blue-trousered Chinese women or little girls in brocaded jackets; and motor-cars, driven by Orientals, honked through this

---

20 Coromandel is a coastal town on the Coromandel Peninsula of New Zealand's North Island. Ceylon is now Sri Lanka.

motley of beings and vehicles with startling incongruity.[21] It was not the Chinese; but I knew that behind this false front, built by homesick exiles, were quarters rich in the atmosphere of Cathay.

I found my way into Queen's Road, one of the main thoroughfares, and there, in a little side street that curved off into fragrant gloom, discovered a flower bazaar. Violets and hyacinths and roses![22] Other blossoms, too, fragile poems whose names I did not know. Generally, I object to buttonhole decorations, whether flowers, flags, or pins; but the heavy sweetness of the curving street, the fresh, moist blossoms, thrice lovely after the bareness of winter Japan, smothered prejudice, and I bought a coral-pink rosebud for my lapel.[23] This fastidious touch seemed, in some mysterious way, to qualify me for adventure.

---

21   The British recruited Sikh males for the Hong Kong Police Force from 1844.

22   I believe Hervey is here referring to Lyndhurst Terrace in Central, which is close to Queen's Road Central and does indeed curve at its junction with Wellington Street. In English the street is named after an English Assistant Magistrate in the colony. However, the street's Cantonese name 擺花 literally means "flower arrangement", presumably due to the historic presence of numerous flower stalls at the junction of Lyndhurst Terrace and Wellington Street.

23   Hervey had visited Japan prior to sailing to Hong Kong.

I followed Queen's Road eastward, absorbing the warm green beauty of luxuriant trees; came at length to numerous barracks and drill grounds. British troopers, tall fellows with sunburnt chests and bare tanned knees, were playing cricket; and I realized how pleasant I was to see soldiers who were not yellow.[24] Beyond the garrison, on a street that sloped up through green shadow, was the terminus of a tramway – the funicular tramway that connected with the Peak. This seemed, suddenly, the place I had been seeking subconsciously, and I boarded a waiting car, taking the front seat, which, a sign informed me, must be surrendered to his Excellency the Governor and his staff should they appear…[25]

---

24   By 'drill grounds' Hervey is here referring to the Parade Ground and the cricket pitch then near the junction of Queen's Road Central and Garden Road.

25   The funicular Peak Tram running from Garden Road in Admiralty to Victoria Peak via the Mid-Levels was opened in 1888. Until 1926 there were three classes of travel – First, for British colonial officials and residents of Victoria Peak; Second, British military and Hong Kong Police Force personnel and; Third, for 'other people and animals'. It was indeed true that, between 1908 and 1949, the first two seats in the front of the tram were reserved exclusively for the Governor of Hong Kong. A bronze plaque read: 'This seat is reserved for His Excellency the Governor'. The seats were not available to ordinary passengers until two minutes before departure.

Not often are my nerves affected by steep grades, yet I confess that I was disturbed as the car, drawn by a slender cable, groaned and screeched up that almost perpendicular incline; indeed I felt actually concerned when it stopped at way-stations and, by merely lowering my eyes, I could look down upon a tiny slanting city that was Hong-kong. However, I managed to observe much of the scenery, the deep pools of greenery from which rose pretentious residencies and over which numerous pink-blossomed trees broke in showers of rose-dyed rain.

The final stop was some distance from the Peak, and I set out on foot, in no wise displeased by the change of locomotion. The road led past the Peak Hotel and upward toward the fogged summit; a steep, winding road that climbed between isolated dwellings and rocky, sparsely grown ravines.[26] As I mounted I could see, over stone walls and descending billows of foliage, a miniature city and harbour below. The wind, sharpened by altitude, drove through my clothes with cruel force; wraiths of mist circled about me, rent into vaporous tatters by the capricious atmosphere. Near the top, which was hooded in fog, I stopped, crouching against a tall rock.

---

26 The Peak Hotel opened for business in 1888 to coincide with the opening of the Peak Tram. The hotel's poor-quality construction meant it never became popular with guests. It was closed in 1936 and destroyed by fire in 1938.

The cold, moist wind struck my face with the force of a damp rag; it swept around the Peak, a palpable wild presence that lashed the mist into fantastic shapes and drove it into gullies and crevices where it lay like cotton wadding. The city and the roadstead, seen between layers of vapour, seemed immeasurably distant and ineffectual; a symbol of the futility of Civilization against the forces of Nature. I felt both exhilarated and depressed. The Peak, in my imagination, became the symbol of China, rising superbly indifferent, above the encroaching sphere of white men; and, suddenly, I felt in close communion with the dreams of a race that had always seemed inscrutable to me. For thousands of years that lofty summit had endured, tortured by wind and storm, gazing upon intrigue and famine and plague and war, yet remaining unaffected beyond minor surface corrosions and a change of exterior appearance with the seasons. Tartar, Mongol, Ming, and Manchu, all had come and gone, each tolerated for a brief period and then crushed. What an impervious monster, this China! Now the victim of internal wars, of jealous Nippon and scheming Occidental nations, would she not endure them for a spell and then... smite them?[27]

I did not stay long in that exalted spot, for the air was too rare, the wind too sharp, and the perspective too vast;

---

27 "Nippon" being Japan.

and when I went down I felt like an ant crawling over some petrified monster.

2.

And now the story of Chang Yuan...

I first saw him in Pennsylvania Station in New York, a slender burnished figure lost in the cold magnificence of marble walls and heavily glassed ceilings. His dark Occidental clothes only accentuated the Oriental mould of his features; smooth, handsome features that in some imperceptible way suggested aristocratic blood. He attracted me instantly, for he should have been robed in plum-coloured silk and borne in a sedan-chair along the streets of some far flowery city. It was only by the chance of twelve letters on my bag that we met. I paused, ostensibly to look at some papers I was carrying but really to study him, perhaps with a view to weaving him into a story, and to my surprise he approached me. He had just arrived from the west, he informed me after apologizing for speaking, and he was to have been met by some one who had not appeared, a gentleman from Philadelphia. As he had seen "Philadelphia" printed on my bag, he presumed that I lived there and wondered if I knew Mr. ___. It was very naïve. And it was the beginning of a brief acquaintance that was delightfully novel. I directed him to a hotel and helped him to find his friend; and before I left the city we dined and went to the theatre together. A most charming person he was, rather poetic, and astonishingly well educated in a Victorian fashion. His home was in Hong-kong, he told me, and he had come to the United States to attend a university for two years; a finishing touch to the education he received at a foreign college in China. After that, he would return home. Should I ever come to Hong-kong I must let him know... His name – well, Chang Yuan.

And so, soon after I arrived in Hong-kong, I wrote him a note; and the following day he appeared, not clad in plum-coloured silk as a I hoped, but wearing a grey European suit. I had feared the effect of a foreign college upon him, but he proved to be the same delightfully archaic person, with only an added air of extreme dignity, faintly grandiose; the result of being in native surroundings again.

That evening we had dinner at a European hotel and afterwards went out to "view the night side of the city," as he expressed it. Red rickshaws whirled us westward along Queen's Road, past the arcaded shops and into the tremulous heat of the native town. In the lighted doorways stood citron-yellow Chinamen; others sat within, smoking and talking; still others lounged on the balconies of the four-storied houses. A stream of people surged in endless procession through the streets. The whisper of bare feet and sandals, the *clap-clap* of leather soles, the ebb and flow of voices, some raucous, some murmurous, melted into a ceaseless muffled clamour; the strange rhythmical restlessness that measures off the dark hours in China and throbs eternally in the memory of those who once hear it. The streets – bright-lanterned thoroughfares, barbaric silk banners and crawling ideographs; narrow side alleys graduated into steps and climbing to who knows what adventures – seemed troughs for this flowing nocturne.

We went to a native theatre first.

"I apologize for bringing you here," said Chang in his dignified manner as we alighted from our rickshaws. "It is a third-class place. I shall take you to a second-class theatre next, then to a first-class. Thus you shall rise by degrees through the Chinese drama and see it in all forms."

The moment our feet touched the pavement beggars besieged us, filthy creatures who materialized from dark corners as if by some horrid sorcery, and came mewling towards us with extended rotted arm-stumps. With an imperial "Chella!" my Chinese friend sent them slinking away, chimeras whose unspeakable deformities haunted me persistently.[28]

---

28   Chella: slang for a lower-class person.

As we entered the theatre, a nauseous effluvia breathed out of the darkness. The odorous gloom was mottled with faces, and beyond the spotted pit that was the audience, in a burst of light from numberless oil-lamps, were creatures so weirdly unreal that they seemed extravagant paper figures cut out of an illustrated book of mythological tales; men with horned helmets and sweeping black beards, accoutred with amazing papier-mâché armour and weapons; and slender porcelain-like women with blanched faces, vermillion lips, and tall auriole-shaped head-dresses.[29] On one side of the stage, incongruously clad in modern dress, where musicians who beat cymbals and drums in a crashing accompaniment to the shrill voices of the actors. There was a grotesque pretence of scenery in a backdrop which was not sufficiently wide and permitted glimpses of mysterious individuals who wandered on and off the rear of the stage. It was all so primitive, so incredibly barbaric, that I was bewildered.

Chang led me down a side aisle, explaining that he was going to initiate me into the back-stage atmosphere of a third-rate theatre. We plunged into a tunnel-like corridor that reeked of latrine smells; mounted slippery stone steps; came out into a dim space lined with curtained stalls. Chang pulled back on the curtains, gesturing contemptuously toward a figure curled up in a bunk.

---

29 Sic – aureole, as in halo shaped.

"They sleep, eat, and live here, like cattle in a stable," he informed me with perceptible disgust. "Indeed, they are not as clean as cattle; they are dung."

In a sphere of fetid gloom behind the backdrop stood a crowd of Chinese watching a performance from the rear; actors were changing their costumes in the orange flare of oil-lights, and I perceived that those whom I had thought women, the vermillion-lipped creatures with the tall aurioles, were young men or boys. I asked Chang if there were no actress in China, and he replied that there were a few, but they were not popular.

"My people," he said, "do not like to see women on the stage, and some even disapprove of their presence in theatres. Many of the new playhouses, like this one, for instance, have special galleries for women, but the older ones have no accommodation for them. I prefer the country theatres," he remarked, "where performances are in the open. This place" – with a deprecating gesture – "is patronized only by common people. The play is cheap – what you call vulgar melodrama. It is a *wu* or military play.[30] That type of performance is always accompanied by much gong-beating."

For a few minutes we watched the exaggerated mimicry of the actors, then retraced our steps through the mottled gloom and out into comparatively clean air.

---

30   *Wu* meaning literally 'martial', 'military', or 'armed'.

The next theatre, although second-class, seemed to me no better than the first; there were the same reeks, the same deafening clamour of cymbals and strident falsetto voices. The third, however, was vastly superior. Both audiences and actors obviously were higher types. The play, Chang explained, was a *p'i-huang,* or musical drama, and was, as always, accompanied by a *lo,* flute, and *hu-Ch'in,* a sort of violin.[31] The costumes were of silk and brocade, and weighted with gold braid and false jewels. The fact that the actors who were supposed to be dead rose and walked off the stage, only one incongruity among many, did not seem to amuse the audience, nor, apparently, even my American-educated host. We stayed through one play which was brief and in two acts. In China, plays generally are very short, and several make up a programme, often each using the same scenery; hence the illusion among the majority of foreigners that Chinese plays, like those of Japan, are interminably long.

After visiting the theatres, we went into Queen's Road West as far as Belcher Street, a quarter which Chang told me was very vicious.[32] And certainly the

---

31   More commonly now a *huqin* traditional bowed string instrument.

32   Actually called Belcher's Street in Kennedy Town, and named after Edward Belcher, a Royal Navy officer who surveyed Hong Kong harbour in 1841.

atmosphere could not be called celestial. There, against a background of brilliantly lighted restaurants and shops, moved the bloated, sensual Chinese merchants of fiction, the cat-like slayers who slither across the pages of scarlet melodrama, and the tiny, rice-powdered, red-lipped girls who, in stories, love and are loved by lily-tongued young Orientals who solve their mutual difficulties – and there are difficulties always – by poisoned wine or some other passport to oblivion. It was a place wickedly thrilling, a quarter such as I had read of in my extreme youth, and it did not fail to supply the necessary touch, an incident of melodramatic realism.

I noticed a crowd gathering at a corner, and I signalled my coolie to stop; Chang did the same. Over the heads of numerous Chinamen I could see two who seemed the centre of attention, tall Mongolian-looking youths who stood facing each other with the calm tenseness that is anger intensified. Behind one was a girl, evidently the cause of the quarrel – a tiny creature with straight black fringe and braided pigtail. For a moment after we paused there was a taut silence; then one of the angry men hissed an anathema which Chang translated.

"Sai-a-nei!"…

"Tue-nei-amah!" whipped back the other.

And then they crashed together in a careening deformity of legs and arms. The crowd receded. I observed a tall Sikh policeman hurrying toward the scene of disturbance. But he was too late. Suddenly one of the fighters vanished from my sight; the other, drawing slobbery breaths, wiped a garnet-red smear from over his eyes, and I saw a knife in his hand... The crowd parted before the towering Sikh.

"Come," Chang urged.

At a command from him the coolies leaped forward, and we were jerked swiftly out of an affair that gave an added sense of uncertainty to the quarter.

We were now in "Kennedy Town," or, as the police know it, District No.1. On either side were four-story buildings, balconied and bannered; and from blazing restaurants came the clashing of cymbals. [33]

Pan-pan-pan-pan-pang! Pan-pan-pan-pan-pang!

They went on without ceasing, clashing and crashing; and their metallic vibrations set the air quivering wildly.

Pan-pan-pan-pan-pang! Pan-pan-pan-pan-pang!

I hear them now, tinkling disks of sound that spin through my memory; and I see the gorgeous wickedness of that quarter; the bursts of orange and crimson light; the gilded façades of the buildings; the little girls in brocaded coats and satin trousers... Mauve and vermillion, azure and sable, gamboge and gold; polychromous confusion...

---

33   Kennedy Town was named after Arthur Edward Kennedy (1809-1883), the seventh Governor of Hong Kong from 1872 to 1877.

It was inevitable that we should visit an opium house. The place was at the end of a slinking alley near the grape-green lamps of Belcher Street; a narrow lane that coiled between high walls and illuminated doorways like a black adder whose poison-fangs were the flame-tongued lights in that "dive" where a few wretches lay drugged in mephitic gloom. The acrid air of the place stung my nostrils; and the soiled bunks, the dirty walls, were cruelly drab. It wasn't picturesquely evil; it was colourless as naked lust; and it left in my brain a negative often developed and printed with tragic sharpness upon my imagination.

Of course, a glimpse of the brothels was included in this excursion.[34] They, like the opium houses, were depressing, tawdry places, opening directly upon the street, with ornate scrolls on the walls and narrow curtained recesses. In each was an altar dedicated to the god of pleasure, and the air was rich with the mingled odours of incense and opium, alive with coiling drifts of blue smoke. The girls, some with spots of scarlet on their eyelids, wore the usual brocaded jackets and trousers. Chang explained, in his grandiose manner, that they were called *loquiia*, and their duties consisted, among other things, of singing and playing to patrons and filling their opium pipes... A

---

34   Brothels were still legally licensed in Hong Kong during Hervey's visit. European-staffed brothels were closed in 1932; Chinese-staffed ones in 1935.

most courteous host, this Chang Yuan, displaying toward the world a lofty superiority and toward me a flattering intimacy. Indeed, in spite of his tweeds, he was a most picturesque person, and I was curious to know something of his manner of living, his environment and intimate thoughts.

It was after midnight when we moved back through Queen's Road West, into the area of the beaten cymbals, and Chang suggested supper at the To-Yuen Restaurant.[35] We were led upstairs by an attendant, past swinging doors and into a private dining-room on the second floor. The walls were over-embellished, the furniture oppressively European. On one side a balcony overhung dark water and the scattered lights of junks and ocean-going craft, and, on the other, windows yielded a view of a wide gallery across the way where marionettes were being worked to attract passers-by and musicians struck cymbals with fiendish persistency. The metallic dissonance had beat itself into my blood, into my brain, and I felt my sanity being pounded to powder. I wondered how I could endure the wild clamour for the length of time required to eat a Chinese meal.

---

35 The To-Yuen Restaurant was located at 420 Des Voeux Road (West) running parallel to Queen's Road. The road is named after the tenth Governor of Hong Kong, Sir William Des Voeux.

"THE TREMULOUS HEART OF THE NATIVE TOWN"

"PAST GILDED, VERMILIONED THEATRES AND GAMBLING-HOUSES MOVED
SLEEPY-EYED BEINGS."

"ENDLESS ROWS OF SHOPS AND DWELLINGS"

41

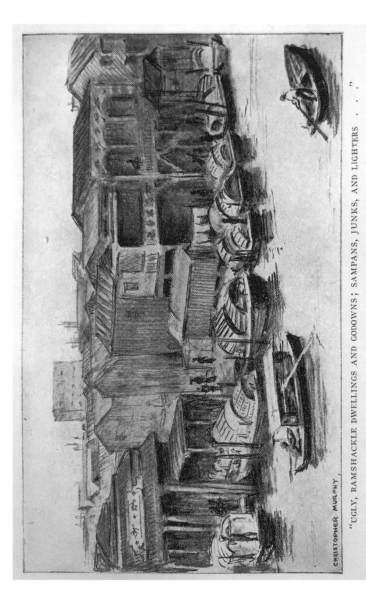

CHRISTOPHER MURPHY.

"UGLY, RAMSHACKLE DWELLINGS AND GODOWNS; SAMPANS, JUNKS, AND LIGHTERS . . ."

"THE FLOWER BOATS . . . LASHED TOGETHER, ELABORATELY CARVED AND GILDED . . ."

RAIN IN CANTON

Chang sent for two singsong girls, which was the proper thing to do, and they arrived coincident with the first course.[36] One was Miss Lai Tsien, and the other Miss Yin Hom; queer, impassive little dolls with straight black fringes cutting severely across the intense pallor of their faces and tiny mouths that suggested slashed crimson berries. Miss Lai Tsien wore a coat of lilac brocade and Miss Yin Hom a jacket of blue silk; and gold ear-rings dripped from their porcelain-pale ears. Singsong girls, like the geisha of Japan, are professional entertainers and are an institution at such restaurants as the To-Yuen. They live in adjacent houses and come at the call of patrons. If a Chinese gentleman wishes to assume intimate relationship with a singsong girl he pays for her service at some restaurant once or twice, and then, when they have become better acquainted, the transaction is concluded at a time and place mutually agreed upon. If, later, he becomes enamoured of her and desires her as his wife or concubine, he buys her from her mistress…

While we consumed innumerable delicacies such as bird's-nest soup, shark's fin, roast duck-skin, and pigeon-eggs, Miss Lai Tsien and Miss Yin Hom stood behind our chairs or sat on the arms and clapped two wooden blocks

---

36 Singsong girls entertained male clients through companionship, singing and dancing and not primarily sexual services (though often this was also the case).

together in sharp accompaniment to falsetto singing; all this given increased barbarity by the infernal and eternal beating of the cymbals. Miss Yin Hom, a charming little creature whose bisque composure sheathed a rather whimsical nature, sang a ballad in Pidgin for my benefit.

> "What-tim he almon' flower hab white when peach-tlee blongey pink,
> My smokey opium-pipe, galaw, an' munchee tim' my tink
> 'Bout all pidgin China-side no fan-kwei[37] understand,
> In olo Fei-Chaw-Shang[38] inside – my nicee Gleen-Tea Land"

Which was explained to me as being "one piece singsong Californee side by China-boy solly inside…"[39]

I regret to say that before we quitted the To-Yuen my host had taken on a distressing quantity of rice-wine.

---

37 *Fan-kwei* (sometimes *fanqui*) meaning 'foreign devils' – i.e. Europeans and Americans.

38 An alternative name for Canton (Guangzhou).

39 This is indeed a real song. The entire song can be found in Charles Godfrey, 'The Green-Tea Land', *Pidgin-English Sing-Song, or Songs and Stories in the China-English Dialect* (London: Kegan Paul, Trench, Trübner & Co. Ltd., 1903). See Appendix I.

But it did not affect his decorum; he was, in fact, more imperial than ever, and he informed me with exaggerated graciousness that I was to be his guest every evening during my stay.

"And before you depart," he added mysteriously, "I shall tell you a story – a story which you must write and call 'Imperial Yellow' – yes, that must be the title; for it is a story of the Forbidden City."

It was something of a shock to see him thus, but his persistent dignity saved me from total disillusion.

About two o'clock we left – to my intense relief. As we came out of the restaurant a boy, his skin mottled by some scrofulous disease, attached himself to us and followed to the rickshaws, making horrible throaty sounds.

"*Fontina*", Chang explained with contempt. "He is crazy."

Then he hissed a few words to the idiot, and the boy, with a terrified glance at the policeman standing at his post in the street, fled, gibbering and screaming, into a side street.

It was a last grim touch to the evening, and the sounds of the idiot's cries, set to the wild crashing of the cymbals, followed me back through muffled streets.

3.

"Politics," declared Chang Yuan, "should never be discussed by friends."

Several nights had passed since our excursion into the Chinese city, and we were seated on the forward deck of the Hong-kong-Kowloon ferry, waiting to be transported to the Victoria shore. Bright star, far-sown over the sky, reaped a harvest in the black harbour below: tiny, twinkling reflections that danced among the tremulous lights of anchored vessels; and the city was a nest of luminous flies whose glowing troops deployed up the mountainside to the very frontier of the stars.

"And yet if I do not speak after you have requested an expression of my views, I shall be guilty of an act of discourtesy," he continued in a manner charmingly Oriental.

"But why do you think I would be displeased by what you have to say?" I pressed.

"The story of Chinese politics is an indictment of Western diplomacy," he replied, simply.

"Of America?"

"No, not of America as a nation, but of the civilization of which she is a part; a civilization that has progressed to an exquisite point in the art of killing; a civilization of Science."

"But China had a civilization when Rome was a barbarian empire," I reminded.

"Yes," he said, "but it was a civilization of Art. It was fundamentally different from Western civilization; different even in small details. For instance, we used, and do use, ideographs instead of an alphabet. In the past, Confucian ethics took the place of religion; that is, among the middle and upper classes. This doctrine, briefly summarized, taught self-restraint, moderation, and courtesy. Our government was a form of patriarchal theism, and the family system was the basis upon which society was built. The governing officials were scholars chosen for their intellectual qualifications; the power of mind was honoured and not the strength of thews and biceps.[40] It was a rule of the *literati*. The West was, and is, the antithesis of this; yet she has always judged China by her own standards. And when China failed to qualify she penalized her – heavily.

"Consider the history of China," he went on.

"Conquered and reconquered, and weakened by international brigandage! The Mongols, the Mings, the Manchus; all have ruled – and have been absorbed. *Absorbed*. You perceive? In the past, when China overthrew her conquerors she did not cast them aside; she assimilated them. It was not strange, then, with such a

---

40   i.e. muscular strength, brawn.

mixture of races, that in 1911, after the revolution, she was stricken with – with national indigestion, as it were. And the medicine of foreign intervention has, unfortunately, done little to relieve the congestion."

He looked at me inquisitively, apologetically, as if expecting me to resent his assertion and pleading innocence of any desire to offend.

"There is always a disorderly element in China," he said when I urged him to go no, "ready to loot and plunder. But generally the various communities can attend to them. However, at present, the people are defenceless against the armed outlawry of the *tuchuns'* armies.[41] The *tuchuns*, you understand, are the military governors. China, of course can only be saved by herself. But the Western powers can assist in the matter of the *tuchuns'* armies; they can demand that these troops disband on the grounds that foreign interests as well as foreign people are being menaced by this continual state of civil war. Thus, with comparatively little effort on the part of the Western nations, China could be rid of one of the evils that block reconstruction. Many prominent officials in both Peking and Canton advocate this move, but they do not publicly declare themselves for fear the Western powers will fail to

41   *Tuchuns* being military governors, or more commonly, warlords.

go through with the programme and they will be left at the mercy of the *tuchuns*." [42]

With a muffled swish and throb the ferry-boat glided away from the landing and toward the shore where Hong-kong hung like a cloud of black mist loaded with fireflies. A damp vapour rising from the channel wrapped me about with silken coolness; it collected in visible aureoles about the deck-lamps and contributed a velvety softness to the surrounding darkness.

Chang Yuan continued:

"There is, paradoxical as it may seem, a fundamental unity among the people because of the fact that about eighty per cent are agriculturalists. Government means to them, not a capital, a president, or an emperor, but the province, the city, and the family – with the family pre-eminent. Even at the time when Manchu despotism was at its height, the wishes of the people were respected; if a viceroy sent by the Dragon Throne was disapproved by the populace he was generally removed. [43] When their household, the sacred institutions of the family, were menaced, they rose. That was the case in 1911 when the Manchus were overthrown. [44] I am a Manchu, but I recognize that their rule had become corrupt. In short,

---

42   Beijing and Guangzhou.

43   i.e. the throne of the Emperor of China.

44   i.e. the *Xinhai*, or Republican, Revolution of 1911.

the dynasty had exhausted the mandate of Heaven. After the revolution, the Emperor was not executed, as would have been the procedure in Europe, but was permitted to remain on the Dragon Throne within the sacred precincts of the Imperial City and supported by an income of four million dollars a year. In fact, it was by a decree of the Throne that the Republic was declared. The President, later, issued a proclamation commanding that his Majesty, a child at the time, be given 'due courtesy, but not fealty and obedience…'[45] Thus custom was preserved without the new rule's being affected, and China became a republic; a republic with an emperor held in reserve.

"Immediately the new regime was established, it borrowed the form of government used by America, not stopping to consider that it might not be consistent with the Chinese character. And the result? We found that a mere change of government was not enough; it had to be a change to a government which the masses could understand and one administered in a way to which they were accustomed. The people, not yet awakened to a centralized authority after years of provincial rule, neglected national interests, mainly because of their ignorance of the new form of government; and corrupt officials took advantage of the situation, misusing their

45 i.e. the Boy, and/or Last, Emperor Puyi (Aisin Gioro Puyi).

power and depleting the treasury and resources of the country. During the presidency of Yuan Shi-k'ai national affairs were comparatively peaceful, but immediately after his attempt to become emperor the present state of perpetual revolution started. That was the beginning of the tyranny of the *tuchuns*.[46]

"You spoke of the 'two governments' when you asked my unworthy opinion of the situation... Ah! If there were only two governments our troubles would be simplified! But there are so many factions: the Peking powers, the Cantonese constitutionalists, the Japanese, the various foreign interests, and numerous small military groups and robber bands. China at present is, indeed, like a great giant tied down by pygmies. That 'great giant' is the people – the men and women who till the soil, who weave and spin, who trade; the millions who know vaguely that there is trouble between North and South, that the Japanese are trying to absorb the country, that foreign greed is adding to the havoc; but who do not understand beyond the mere realization that the sacred institutions of the family are being threatened. When

---

46 More commonly spelt Yuan Shih-kai (1859-1916), a military and government official in the late Qing dynasty who established the first modern Chinese army. Yuan became the first official president of the Republic of China in 1912. He died while still in office and having declared himself Emperor in March 1916.

they are awakened – and they are stirring now, harried by soldiers and brigands – the giant will rise and crush its pygmy tormentors. Without a leader, however, that effort will result only in more chaos, and ultimately China will be dominated by Japan or become a vassal of Western powers."

We were in mid-channel; and, in front, the Peak rose out of the nebulous vapour that was Hong-kong burying its crest in gloom. Again, as on the day of my arrival, it seemed a symbol of China, a great monster brooding over an encroaching civilization. It was incredible that such a Cyclops should ever become enslaved.

"Under a dictator," Chang explained, "some one man forceful enough to destroy the tyranny of bureaucracy. China could be given a breathing-spell in which to build up her finances and heal the wounds left by internal wars; and thus developed by her own people and transformed from a collection of feudatory provinces into a united nation, she would be sufficiently strong to combat Japanese oppression alone. When I say 'combat' I do not mean to fight actually, for it is my unworthy opinion that China united would be formidable enough to dissipate Japan's dream of expansion in Asia. The difficulty at present is in finding the proper man. It is interesting to conjecture who he might be. One of the *tuchuns* themselves? There are several eligible. General Wu Pei Fu,[47] the liberal military leader, is master of the Yang-tse[48] section and a powerful figure in northern politics. He and Chang Tso-lin[49] fought the An Fu Club[50] together, but later they broke and became enemies. In fact, Wu forced Chang to resign from his post as inspector-general of Manchuria. Chang is trying to reassert his power, but he will never have the support of the people, for he was a *hung-hu-tzee* – an outlaw – and rose to eminence through Japanese influence.

47 Wu Pei-fu (1874-1939), was a key figure in the northern warlord struggles between 1916-1927. His armies were overrun by Chiang Kai-shek in the 1927 Northern Campaign to suppress the warlords and unite China under the Kuomintang (KMT).

48 More commonly Yangtze, referring to the river and surrounding country.

49 Chang Tso-lin, or more commonly now Zhang Zuolin (1875-1928), was a Manchurian warlord between 1916 and 1928 also commonly known as the Old Marshal and the Tiger of Mukden (Shenyang). Zhang gained control of Beijing in April 1926. However, he was defeated by Chiang Kai-shek in May 1928 and then assassinated by a bomb planted by the Japanese Kwantung Army in June 1928.

50 The An Fu Club, better known now as the Anhui Clique, was a military and political faction in the Warlord era. It was named after Anhui province because several of its generals, including its founder, Duan Qirui, were from Anhui.

"In the South, Cheng Chiung Ming is an important general.[51] At one time he and Sun – Dr. Sun Yat Sen – were allied, but it is reported tat Sun dismissed him; whatever the cause, the fact remains that they are no longer colleagues. If Sun fails, Cheng will undoubtedly swing into greater prominence in the South. Sun is an enigma. Some say he is an opportunist; others declare he is an ardent patriot. Who knows the truth? There have been rumours of an agreement between him and Chang Tso-lin. If this is true he will lose much support.

"When speaking of the North a moment ago, I neglected to mention Tsao Kun, the President.[52] But he is an unlikely prospect, as it is well known that he is a tool of the powers. That finishes the list of possible dictators. There is, however, another force to be considered, a monarchist element whose hopes are invested in the young emperor.[53] While he is virtually a prisoner in the Imperial Palace, his influence extends over a great portion

---

51 More commonly Chen Chiung-ming or Chen Jiongming (1878-1933).

52 More commonly known as General Cao Kun (1862-1938), a Chinese warlord and politician from 1923 to 1924, as well as the military leader of the Zhili Clique in the Beiyang Army. He became the sixth President of the Republic of China for a year between October 1923 and October 1924 (and so therefore the President of China during Hervey's visit).

53 i.e. Puyi, the Last Emperor.

of the North and even down into the South. The people have not forgotten that he is Lord of Ten Thousand Years; and reports from within the Forbidden City say that he is vitally interested in politics and is an extremely capable boy. In the event of all other mans failing to cast off the *tuchuns*, there will undoubtedly be an attempt to invest his Majesty with the actual power of his office. And I am not sure that the country might not rally under the Dragon Flag...

"And so you perceive that the problems of China are many. In the interior if the Great Wall, and along the coast is the wall of foreign influence; one a symbol of the past, the other a threat of the future. Hong-kong" – with a gesture toward the climbing lights – "is one of the turrets, so to speak, in that alien bulwark. Its acquisition by the British was no worse than similar seizures made by other nations; it is simply an example of the international piracy that China has suffered for two centuries. Some time before 1842 certain British traders living at Canton were persecuted by the citizens and driven out. They fled to Macao, but ill-feeling persisted, and they were forced to take refuge at Hong-kong. It was all very deplorable, but the penalty was too severe. Promptly the island was occupied by an expeditionary force; and at the end of hostilities it was granted to England.

"That was in 1842. Ten or twelve years later France and England together made war on China, and during the fighting at Peking their troops destroyed the Summer Palace, an edifice as magnificent as a cathedral demolished in the recent European War.[54]

"There was nothing to justify this act of barbarism. It was simply part of the ruthless enforcement of the civilization of Science upon the civilization of Art. As a consequence of that war, seven more ports were opened to trade, also along the Yang-tse[55]; a huge indemnity was

---

54　The Great War of 1914-1918 (and after 1945 of course, the First World War).

55　The 1842 Treaty of Nanking (Nanjing) following the First Opium War (1839-1842) established five (rather than seven) treaty ports, in addition to ceding the island of Hong Kong in perpetuity to Great Britain at Shanghai, Canton (Guangzhou), Ningpo (Ningbo), Fuchow (Fuzhou), and Amoy (Xiamen). Other treaty ports were created at later dates. According to the Treaty of Nanking the Qing government was obliged to pay the British government 6,000,000 silver dollars for the opium that had been confiscated by Viceroy Lin Zexu in 1839 (Article IV), 3,000,000 silver dollars in compensation for debts that the *Hong* (or large business) merchants in Canton owed British merchants (Article V), and a further 12,000,000 silver dollars in war reparations for the cost of the war (Article VI). The total sum of 21,000,000 dollars was to be paid in instalments over three years and the Qing government would be charged an annual interest rate of five per cent for the money that was not paid in a timely manner (Article VII).

paid, and more territory was ceded to Great Britain – namely Kowloon.[56]

"The enforcement continued. Later an Englishman was murdered through no fault of the Government, and because of his death an indemnity together with a fixed tariff was obtained… Then the French seized Annam[57]… Britain took Burma.[58] Both belonged to the ancient Empire.[59] Then came the war with Japan, the loss of Korea, of Manchuria.[60] Later, two German missionaries were killed in Shan-tung.[61] Accordingly, Germany

---

56 In 1860 the Kowloon Peninsula was ceded to Great Britain in perpetuity.

57 The central portion of what is now Vietnam and incorporated into the French Indo-Chinese Empire in 1887.

58 Burma (Myanmar) was annexed by Britain in January 1886 and was incorporated into the British Indian Raj.

59 Meaning here the ancient empire of China.

60 The First Sino-Japanese War (1894-1895) was fought between the Qing Empire and the Empire of Japan, primarily for influence over Korea. The Qing vassalage over Korea's Joseon dynasty was ended and Korea became incorporated into Japan's sphere of influence. China was also forced to cede the Liaodong Peninsula in south-eastern Manchuria to Japan following the by the Treaty of Shimonoseki in April 1895.

61 The so-called Juye Incident where two German Catholic missionaries, Richard Henle and Franz Xaver Nies, of the Society of the Divine Word, were murdered in Juye County Shan-tung (Shandong) province, in November 1897. A third missionary, Georg Maria Stenz, survived the attack unharmed. Less than

claimed Kaio-chau Bay and secured railway and mining interests in the province where the two missionaries were murdered... Even Russia came in for her share in the Empire: she made a naval base out of Port Arthur[62]; and England, not to be outdone, took Wei-hai-wei..."[63]

We had reached the Hong-kong docks, and the tawny lights of the city stretched away on either side, like flecks of rust on a sheet of gun-metal. The ferry-boat warped in with a great churning of water.

"As a climax," said Chang Yuan, rising, "came the Boxer rebellion, and the Allies sacking Peking, demanded and received large indemnity, and further intrenched themselves in China by turning the Legation Quarter into a fortified city... And thus," he finished in his polite,

---

two weeks after the Juye Incident, the German Empire used the murders of the missionaries as a pretext to seize Kiao-chau (Jiaozhou) Bay on Shandong's southern coast.

62   Now Lushun, and formerly seized by Czarist Russia in the 1904-1905 Russo-Japanese War. Lushun is now a district of the city of Dalian in Liaoning province.

63   In eastern Shandong province Wei-hai-wei, or more commonly Weihaiwei (and sometimes Port Edward) was under British rule from July 1898, under lease agreement with the Qing government. Today it is referred to as Weihai.

imperial manner, "was proved the superiority of Science over Art." [64]

4.

Evidently Chang Yuan's extravagant assertion that I was to be his guest every evening was not the result of too much rice-wine, or, if it was, he was sufficiently sober to realize what he was saying and later make good his words. Each afternoon at tea-time he appeared, suggesting some new expedition; in fact, his invitations were so numerous, his

---

64   The Boxer Uprising of 1900 and subsequent siege of the foreign legations led to the dispatch of the so-called Eight Powers Allied Army (comprised of Japan, Russia, Britain, France, the United States, Germany, Italy and Austria-Hungary) who sacked and looted Peking. The September 1901 Boxer Protocol between the Qing government and the eight nations included reparations to be paid by China of 450,000,000 *taels* of silver. The reparation was to be paid within 39-years and would be 982,238,150 *taels* with interest (four per cent per year) included. China continued to pay the reparation until 1939. The Legation Quarter was rebuilt with gates on three sides manned by various foreign troops. The fourth side was the Tartar Wall. Chinese access was severely limited; passes were required; foreign troops were stationed within the Quarter and a glacis (an open piece of land which exposes attackers to the defenders' missiles) was built to the eastern side of the Quarter.

hospitality so prodigal, that I was embarrassed. However, I realized that it was an example of true Eastern graciousness, and to have refused would have been regarded, by him, as an expression of discourtesy. Chang, like all high-class Chinese, was quite punctilious in the matter of etiquette. His early training according to Confucian methods, particularly the custom of self-effacement, had survived more than two years spent in the West. Indeed, I was surprised that he persisted in wearing European clothes. In his dress he was exquisite, and I could imagine that, had he chosen to effect native costume, his appearance would have been elegant in the extreme. His tweed suits never ceased to irritate me.

He was exceptionally friendly, and we discussed a diversity of subjects with freedom: yet always I felt that was withholding his actual thoughts, that he would never be wholly candid because of the ineffaceable fact that I was a white man. Whenever he spoke of his family it was in a rather indefinite way; only once did he refer to his home, and then his remarks was merely a vague hint that he lived somewhere among the mountainside villas hanging over Hong-kong. This, together with his lavish expenditure of money, indicated that he was wealthy; and my fancy pictured his father as a retired court official who had escaped the revolution with a fortune squeezed from the people during the despotic latter years of the

Manchu dynasty.[65] Chang became, in my eyes, a most mysterious figure; mysterious, not inscrutable. For he was not enigmatical, as the Chinese are believed to be; he was simply uncommunicative – the inevitable Oriental accepting the foreigner with reservations.

Three days before I was to leave Hong-kong, Chang invited me to go to Macao, an old Portuguese-Chinese city on the island of Heung Shan, some forty miles across the estuary of the Canton River.[66] The name 'Macao,' or, to give the town its full title, 'Cidade do Santo Nom de Deus de Macao,' has always held a wicked allurement for me… Baize-topped tables; clinking cash; the opulent fume of poppy-smoke… It is there that the most notorious gambling-houses in the Orient slumber by day and purr by night. And from the great brass cauldrons of its opium factories pours a ceaseless stream of black treacle that flows around the world…[67]

---

65   i.e. the Qing dynasty.

66   Hervey appears to be slightly confused here. The Heung Shan he is referring to is most probably the more commonly spelt Heung-san ("Fragrant Mountain") and now the city called Zhongshan (named after Dr. Sun Yat-sen, or Sun Zhongshan in modern Mandarin). It is downriver from Guangzhou and close to Macao.

67   Cidade do Santo Nom de Deus de Macao being City of the Holy Name of God of Macao.

From Hong-kong to Macao is a three- or four-hour run; and our ship, a steamer that made regular trips, shook off the mist of Victoria, like a moth discarding a damp cocoon, and luxuriated in the golden splendour of a sun-warmed sea. Forward, iron grilles protected the companionway of the engines. These, Chang explained, were a precaution against pirates. Only a week or two before, he went on to day, a boat coming in from the Portuguese colony had been seized, the passengers locked on the cabins, and the ship looted and set adrift... It sounded rather splendid; indeed, I could fancy the exquisite thrill put into motion by the sudden appearance of a pirate junk on that agate smooth sea.

On the lower deck were numberless coolies, the majority naked to the waist, their great salient muscles given an oily glisten by the sunlight; all bound for the gambling colony, inflamed by dreams of fan-tan and opium and little girls with blood carmine lips… Bare-breasted islands lay drowsing in the pure silence: flecks of dust on a great, flawless blue pearl... There was, on our deck, a Chinaman clothed after the manner of a Cantonese gentleman. He wore a long black robe, slashed at the sides and buttoned, and a black silk skullcap. Under the outer garment was a full blue skirt. His Oriental attire gave him a dignity that even Chang, with all his regal manners, could not equal; and I remarked to my friend that I rather fancied the native dress of his country. He seemed surprised.

"Yes? Had I known that, I would not have changed to European clothing. You see," he explained, "it is – how do the French say it? – *défendu*? – it is *défendu* for a white man to associate with a Chinese gentleman in Hong-kong; at least, according to the British. So, for your sake, I cast aside my national costume temporarily." [68]

I felt that I knew him well enough to discuss a delicate matter, and so I dropped a probing question in regard to the relationship between white and yellow in Hong-kong.

"Analysed, it is simply a matter of the difference in the colour of the skin," he said, candidly. "Coolie or high official, the discrimination, fundamentally, is slight. Socially, in diplomatic circles, the high official is accepted, but one Englishman never fails to apologize to the other for the fact. Race-consciousness is very highly developed in the British – but no more than in the Chinese. We have not forgotten our heritage."

Macao first appeared as ivory-pale blur in the blue haze; then gradually I seemed carved out of the misty diffusion of reflected sunlight, asserting itself in green and silver substantiality – a semicircle of pygmy houses and

---

68   *Défendu* – literally 'forbidden', but perhaps in this context more akin to the English phrase 'not quite the done thing'.

gardens overlooking a half-moon bay. On a full-bosomed promontory at one end of the town stood a lighthouse, an immaculate sentinel poised above the mellow-hued stucco buildings.

Immediately upon landing we took rickshaws along the Praia Grande and through the European and Chinese quarters. In the former were many splendid dwellings and gardens thick with subtropical plants; many fountains, too, gurgling and fuming in the voluptuous sunshine. A rather sensuous place, this Macao. Particularly the Chinese quarter. Through narrow, tortuous streets and between low houses; past gilded, vermilioned theatres and gambling-palaces moved sleepy-eyed beings, some of whom were pure Chinese or Portuguese but most of whom where Nhons; that is to say, a mixture of both. These Nhons, said Chang, speak a Portuguese *patois* and call themselves subjects of Portugal; in fact, many full-blooded Chinese do the same for business reasons.[69]

As we rode through the town that afternoon, I was surprised to see a familiar black-swathed figure moving

69   'Nhon' being a rather dated term for mixed-race Macanese or Eurasian. Macanese Patois (known as *Patuá* to its speakers) is a Portuguese-based creole language with a substrate from Malay, Cantonese and Sinhalese, which was originally spoken by the Macanese (or as Hervey would have it, Nhon) community of Macao. It is now spoken by very few people in Macau and in the Macanese diaspora and is on the endangered languages list.

sombrely against a moss-grown wall – a Christian nun. Her shadow wavered along the street behind her, frail as an illusion; and in the brutal white glare she looked so pallid, her skin so transparent, that she seemed more like a symbol than a woman; a symbol that, in this yellow country, was an expression of tragic futility... And just before dusk (the sky becoming a brilliant hue) I heard the pealing of chimes: transparent rose-petals of sound that scattered through the dying sunset and withered. There was something wistful and lonely in the music, a note mournfully intimate, and it took me back to my own country, to a little town in the mountains, where each autumn the forests rust and die, and cathedral chimes toll heartbreaking melancholy...

After nightfall, when a tiara of lights crowned the bay, Chang led the way to a very exclusive establishment where glazed-paper lanterns, heavily ideographed, proclaimed its purpose. The interior presented a scene soaked in thick aqueous blue smoke and enriched by the pungent odour of opium. Around a large table on the lower floor were crowds of middle-class Chinese, swimming in the weird smoke-light like the inhabitants of some undersea cavern. Above, hovering over the encircling rail of a gallery, was a multitude of faces floating in the gloom like misshapen moons. There, said Chang, indicating the faces, were the high-class patrons. Accordingly, we joined them, escorted thither by an attendant. A most elegant assembly crowded this upper floor, all men, and dressed in silks and brocades, some standing by the rail, lowering their bets to the table below by the means of a basket, and other lounging upon divans, drinking tea or inhaling poppy-smoke. The air staggered with the combined richness of opium-fumes and pomaded humanity.

Several Chinese gentlemen politely made room for us at the rail, and we gazed down at the beings who swarmed around the table. Piles of coins glimmered through the blue smoke, like sunken treasure. Moving lithely among the gamblers were satin-trousered courtesans who now and then lifted blanched faces to us. It looked very wicked and very pleasant, and it stung my blood with challenge. Many times during the following two hours I lowered the basket and drew it up empty; and many times Chang ordered whisky-sodas...

Somewhere near midnight (I am sure it was midnight, for that is the propitious hour for bizarre happenings) Chang suggested repairing to a private room where he had ordered supper to be served; the cook connected with this establishment prepared a faultless birds'-nest pudding... In the room were two ebony divans, and Chang explained that frequently patrons remained overnight. A window opened toward the sea, which was hidden behind roofs, and in the soft darkness that thickened above the reflected glare of the street-lamps were sprinkled the phosphorescent ashes of stars.

My host insisted on having whisky and soda with the supper. It was rather distressing, as long ago I had ceased to count the drinks he had taken. In justice to him, however, I must add that he contained them with astonishing ease. Oh, a magnificent personage, this Chang Yuan! He was like a figure out of Romance; and he remained so until the end…

Suddenly, and quite abruptly, he drew a photograph from his inside pocket and extended it to me.

"This is my grandmother," he said, simply.

It was a picture that I had seen often, that I recognized instantly. Sitting on a throne, against the background of a magnificently carved screen and flanked by tall peacock-feather fans, was an austere old woman, wearing full embroidered robes and a *Gu'un Dzan*, as a Manchu lady's head-dress is called.

"I see," I commented politely, tasting of bitter disillusion, for I had never expected to behold Chang Yuan in a state of such lofty intoxication that he would claim the late Empress Dowager as his grandmother![70]

70 The Empress T'zu Hsi An, now more commonly Cixi (1835-1908) had been chosen as a concubine of the Hsien-Feng (Xianfeng) Emperor as a girl. She had borne him a son in 1856. After the Hsien-Feng Emperor's death in 1861, the

"I carry it with me always," he explained, quite seriously, "as a talisman. It brings me good luck."

He leaned across the table, in his sloe-black eyes the first animation I had ever seen him display.

"Do you remember I said that I had a story for you?... Well, I shall tell you it now; and some time you must write it and call it 'Imperial Yellow.' Will you? You promise?... And you will promise also," he pursued, "that my name shall never be mentioned?... I trust you. You are my friend. That is why I tell you this. I am a descendent of the Yehonala clan, which began in the region of the Long White Mountain, the cradle of Manchu aristocracy.[71] Lao Tzu Sang, the Great Ancestor" – gesturing toward the photograph, lying face upward on the table – "was my grandmother. But my grandfather was not the Emperor, her husband, Hsien-Feng. I do not know who

---

young boy became the Tongzhi Emperor, and she became the Empress Dowager. Cixi ousted a group of regents appointed by the late emperor and assumed regency, consolidating control over the Qing dynasty when she installed her nephew as the Guangxu Emperor at the death of her son in 1875. Both Cixi and the Guangxu Emperor died in 1908 leaving the Manchu court in the hands of conservatives and a child, Puyi, on the throne for the last years of the Qing dynasty.

71　Empress Dowager Cixi was originally from the Manchu Yehonala clan (or the Manchu Bordered Yellow Banner Yehe Nara clan) and, when younger, was sometimes known in the Forbidden City as Yehonala.

my grandfather was. Perhaps Jung Lu, an officer of the Imperial Guards[72]; or the eunuch An Ti-hai, who was not a eunuch[73]; of Li Lien-ying, who also falsely called himself a eunuch.[74] I cannot say which. But my father

---

72 Cixi is believed to have had a relationship, possibly sexual, with Jung Lu, who commanded the Guangxu Emperor's troops and, later (after some political manoeuvring by Cixi), his palace guard too. Jung Lu was notoriously devoted to Cixi.

73 An Ti-hai (or alternatively An Te-hai and now An Dehai) was born in 1844 and brought up in Beijing in a poor family that compelled him, at the age of twelve, to become a eunuch. He became powerful within the Forbidden City due to his closeness to Cixi as her personal attendant and referred to as "Little An" by her. He became central to a power struggle in the court between Cixi and Prince Gong. In open violation of palace rules An regularly left the confines of the Forbidden City and Beijing. For this he was beheaded in 1869 and his relatives banished to the far north of China. Though the Empress Dowager appears to have been smitten with An and An did take a wife there is no serious evidence that he was not in fact a eunuch and so therefore Chang Yuan and his father's theory that An Dehai was a false eunuch is not correct.

74 Li Lien-ying (Li Lianying), a palace eunuch, was born in 1848 and died in 1911. He was very close to Cixi as an adviser, especially after the execution of An Ti-hai. He became known officially as the Grand Supervisor. There is some suspicion that it was Li that poisoned the Guangxu Emperor in 1908. Li retired after the death of Cixi and died shortly before the fall of the Qing dynasty. Once again, despite rumours that swirled around pretty much all the most powerful eunuchs in

believes that the head eunuch, An Ti-hai, fathered him into existence. Perhaps."

I knew that there was gossip about the late Empress Dowager and her two head eunuchs, An Ti-hai and Li Lien-ying; also I was a well-known and widely chronicled fact that her majesty had been enamoured of her handsome young guardsman Jung Lu. Indeed, there was talk (and writing, too) of a child that had been smuggled out of the Forbidden City… But Chang Yuan! The faultless Chang Yuan! Surely he was drunk or romancing….

A "boy" brought more whisky and another siphon, and Chang Yuan drank. The expression in his eyes had become hazy and introspective. It may have been only an illusion, but I thought I saw him sway slightly.

"Grandson of her Majesty T'zu Hsi An, Empress of the West," he resumed, fingering his glass.[75] "She was called Lao Fu Yeh, the Great old Buddha.[76] Women are not often great. But Yehonala, the Old Buddha… She began her career as a concubine; and when she died her full title was T'zu-Hsi-Tuan-yu-K'ang-yi-Chao… Chao-

the Forbidden City, there is no evidence that Li was a false eunuch.

75 Tzu Hsi (or more commonly now Cixi) means "empress of the western palace", a title given her as she because she lived inside the western Chuxiu Palace in the Forbidden City.

76 Lao Fu Yeh (or Lao Fo-yeh) is the Chinese for 'great old Buddha', hence Cixi's nickname.

yu-Chang-Shou-kung-Ch'in-hsien" – a pause – "Ch'ang-hsi-Hu-ang-Tai-Hou."

He finished with triumphant smile, while I, in abject humility, marvelled at his ability to remember the title after drinking so many whisky sodas.

"A very great woman," he repeated. "The story must be about her mainly – about her life – and it must be called 'Imperial Yellow.' I should like to write it, but I... I am not a scholar; indeed, no, I would not be capable. But you; you must do it; you, my friend... The story of Yehonala... of her son by Jung Lu or An Ti-hai or Li Lien-ying... and of her grandson... Three generations... a royal romance."

He took another drink. The misty look had vanished from his eyes, and he was smiling in his cordial yet reserved manner.

"I must tell you how she came to the Forbidden City," he continued. "It will explain one of the customs of the Manchu dynasty. When the Emperor Tao-Kung died – ascended the Dragon, as we say – Hsien-Feng succeeded him as the Son of Heaven and the Lord of Ten Thousand Years.[77] When the period of mourning for the old Emperor was over – twenty-seven months is the proper

---

77   Tao-kung, known as the Daoguang Emperor (1782-1850), who ruled from 1820 to 1850. Succeeded by Hsien-Feng, the Xianfeng Emperor.

time – a decree was issued commanding all beautiful and aristocratic Manchu girls to appear at the palace for selection for the imperial harem... Yehonala was chosen as the concubine and became *Kuei Jen*, meaning Honourable Person. She was clever, oh, clever; and from the very start, it is said, she knew that she would become a great woman. She worked herself into the good graces of the late Emperor Tao-kung's widow, who was nominally the head of the house; and that influence, particularly after the birth of the heir apparent, cemented her power.[78] She practically ruled the empire when she was twenty-two years old; for the Emperor was weak and dissolute, and the Empress Consort took no interest in politics...

"A house-law of the dynasty forbade the administration of government by a female – but what was that to Yehonala? She always found some subterfuge that assuaged public opinion. She was supreme – supreme until the end. She conquered all. Her one son, the Emperor Tung-chih[79], she destroyed by encouraging him to lead a vicious life; and she caused his wife, A-lu-te, to commit suicide directly after giving birth to an heir.[80] Nor did she let the

---

78   The "widow" being. the Empress Dowager Cixi.

79   Better known as the Tongzhi Emperor (1856-1875) who reigned from 1861 to 1875.

80   A-lu-te, or more commonly known as Lady Arute or the Empress Xiaozheyi (1854-1875). The circumstances

child rule, but appointed the son of one of the Manchu princes. The boy became emperor, but in title only, for the Old Buddha, who dominated him from the very first, never permitted him to have a great amount of power. Once he tried to overthrow her; and the result... he was imprisoned on an island in the palace grounds, and there he died – of poison – within twenty-four hours of the old Buddha's death... Oh, a terrible woman, my friend, a magnificent woman!" [81]

---

surrounding the Xiaozheyi Empress's death are unclear. Following the death of the Tongzhi Emperor at just eighteen years of age without naming a successor. Without consulting A-lu-te, the Empress Dowager Cixi made the decision that her three-year-old nephew Zaitian would be enthroned as the Guangxu Emperor. Cixi also denied A-lut-te the customary title of Empress Dowager. It is generally believed that A-lu-te committed suicide due to persecution from Cixi. It was widely believed that A-lu-te was pregnant at the time of her death with the child that, if male, would have been the heir to the Dragon throne.

81   The Guangxu Emperor lived in the Yingtai Pavilion, a palace on a lake that is now part of the Zhongnanhai Compound following the failed reforms of the Hundred Days Reform Movement in 1898. It does seem that the Guangxu Emperor was poisoned in 1908 and died a day before Cixi. It is still not entirely clear who poisoned the Emperor – Cixi herself or the military moderniser who was close to Cixi (and later to become President, and for a short time Emperor, of China himself), Yuan Shi-kai.

Again, the rheumy expression clouded his eyes. The bottle of whisky was half empty…

"It will make a splendid story," he went on, "beginning with her life and ending with mine. I shall give you the details. Bu the most interesting part will be the first: telling of the Old Buddha's life in the Forbidden City… in the Summer Palace. Let Jung Lu, the officer of the Imperial Guard, be the hero; say that he was my grandfather. I have heard that he was a very handsome and scholarly person; and I do not like the thought of being the descendant of a sham eunuch. No, it must be Jung Lu in the story… Let them sail on the Lotus Lake on moonlight nights; or walk up Peony Hill[82]; or meet on the Jade Girdle Bridge[83]… They are such pleasant names… the Jade Girdle Bridge… the Spreading Cloud Pavilion[84]… the Pavilion of Purple Light…"[85]

---

82 Hervey here most probably means Jingshan Park, which was originally named Wansui Hill (Long Live Hill), Zhen Hill or Meishan Hill (Coal Hill) that overlooks the Forbidden City towards the north.

83 More commonly known as the Jade Belt Bridge or the Camel's Back Bridge, located on the grounds of the Summer Palace.

84 Most probably Hervey is referring to the Baoyunge (or Pavilion of Precious Clouds) in Beijing's Summer Palace.

85 Here Hervey means the Ziguangge, otherwise known usually as the Purple Light Pavilion or the Violet Light Tower,

Once more I thought I saw him sway. His chin was in his hands, and he looked ahead without seeing me. Hastily I prompted him; I asked how the story would continue, how it would end. He gazed at me blankly for a moment, then smiled, that kingly, reserved smile.

"Oh, the end" – and I was positive that he swayed then – "yes, the end… But perhaps I could tell you the end more clearly in the morning," he said politely, apologetically. "I am somewhat fatigued. You will pardon me if I suggest that we retire?"

He rose with exaggerated dignity and managed to reach one of the divans. I believe he fell asleep instantly.

5.

And that is the end.

Two days later I sailed for Manila. Chang was at the dock, as charmingly dignified and regal as ever. I had hoped that he might appear in native dress, the plum-coloured robe of my fancy; but he wore faultless grey tweeds and the crease in his trousers stood out like a sabre's edge. He had not once referred to his indiscretion in Macao

---

located in Zhongnanhai to the western side of the Forbidden City.

(certainly I had not), nor did he speak of them at the last moment as I expected he would, his only remark was:

"You must be sure to send me a copy of your book."

And I shall…

WHERE STRANGE GODS CALL

(II)

THE CITY OF SOMBRE FACES:
CANTONESE FRAGMENTS

1.

I left Kowloon on a slate-coloured day in March. A fine diamond-drizzle sprinkled the decks of the *Kinshan*; the wind, packed with the dregs of frost, twisted the air and whipped the tarpaulins covering the hatches.[86] Behind, as we throbbed out into the harbour, the mountains of Victoria Island looked like a line of great grey camels in the mist.

---

86 The steamer *Kinshan* (1903-1942) sailed between Hong Kong, Macao and Canton, a joint service of the Hong Kong, Canton and Macao Steamship Co. Ltd and the China Navigation Co. Ltd.

Guards patrolled the decks, lithe yellow chaps in soiled uniforms. As on the steamship to Macao, iron bars laced the companionways communicating with the engine-room... The river-pirates, volunteered an optimistic Eurasian at my side, had been particularly bold of late. Had I heard what happened to the Macao boat recently? Yes? Well, that was only one among many similar depredations. Pirates were thick as lice along the Pearl River; many nested in the old forts that pierced the deserted shores like rotten honeycombs.[87] Elusive, impudent vermin, these river buccaneers. They were rarely caught because most of the native officials and police were pirates themselves. But now and then, for the sake of appearances, a band was brought to justice. Some were tortured with the rope before execution; others were places in a tall wooden frame that just permitted their toes to touch the ground, and they hung there until they turned purple; but the majority were beheaded immediately. There was a place in Canton where such executions could be seen, he informed me. And, really, they were quite a sight. A rope was twisted around the condemned man's neck, and he was jerked forward into a kneeling position; then, *quish!* went the blade, and his head slobbered across the ground in a welter of blood....

---

87 Also at the time known as the Canton River, and now more commonly as the Zhujiang.

The river trip was invested with a mild uncertainty as a consequence of the Eurasian's talk. But I saw no pirates; only barren, hilly shores; at times patterned with passing junks or other queer Chinese craft; a few desolate forts; scattered villages; and, as we neared Canton, two slender-spired pagodas that seemed to pin up the low clouds.

Some cities, like unpleasant events, cast a warning before them. One approaches them with foreboding, aware that they are woven into one's destiny with a dark and dreadful thread... As we pressed closer to Canton I felt the luxuriousness inspired by Hong-kong giving away to a melancholy profound as the rain-packed sky overhead. I knew, intuitively, that the Canton of my boyhood fancies – a place of royal purple, of the grandeur of gold lacquer screens and dragon tapestries – was about to betray me to a reality.

This premonition was verified as the houses multiplied, and suddenly, too suddenly, we were gliding past ugly, ramshackle dwellings and go-downs; grass-thatched house-boats, sampans, junks, and lighters, and millions of roofs that were flung in uneven terraces against the sky.[88] The piles of houses, the swarming river and docks, instantly gave me a sense of tremendous and baffling energy. Canton was at once, and always will be, too stupendous and too indefinite to be sheathed in words.

---

88   Go-downs being warehouses.

From the wharf – a roofed landing stage thronging with curious yellow mortals – I was rickshawed violently over the bridge and upon Shameen, an island south-east of the old and new cities, where the Europeans live.[89] There I found myself in another world, a pleasant if somewhat conventional sphere of brick houses, sidewalks, and lush camphor-trees and banyans that cast a green dusk.

The quiet of Shameen, after the confusion of the river-front, gave me an opportunity to recover my equilibrium, and by the time I reached the hotel I was in the mood for exploration.[90] A morose-looking individual in a *tai-check-sam*, as the long coat of the Chinese gentleman is called, took charge of me shortly after my arrival, informing me that one could not go through the naïve city without a guide. I demanded to know the reason, for I detested the idea of being conducted. Well, he replied, the sedan-chair coolies did not speak English, and one could easily become lost in the maze of narrow streets. Indeed, yes! One might

89 Shameen, or now more commonly Shamian, is a sandbank island. Shameen literally means "sandy surface" in Chinese. The territory was divided into two concessions given to France and Britain by the Qing government in the nineteenth century. Shameen was connected to the mainland by two bridges: the British arch bridge, also called the "Bridge of England" built in 1861, and the French bridge to the east.

90 Hervey must have stayed in the Victoria Hotel as it was, at the time, the only such establishment on Shameen.

be robbed; one might be held for ransom; or one might even be killed! Canton was a city of chaos those days. The Kwangtung,[91] Dr. Sun's troops, were in control, but there was a report that the rebellious Kwang-si might attack at any moment.[92] So, he concluded, I could see why it was necessary for me to have a guide, and particularly such a thorough guide as himself.

2.

We left Shameen by the Yuenhang Gate. There are two gates, each on a bridge, one linking the island with Nam-kwan and the other with Sai-kwan.[93] Every evening at six o'clock these gates were closed, my guide told me as we rocked over a murky canal in sedan-chairs; after that no Chinaman went on to Shameen without a pass and no European entered the native town unescorted.[94]

"Murder and pillage occur every night," he added, gloomily. "The soldiers are mercenaries, hired by petty *tuchuns* – military governors, you understand. Kwang-

---

91   i.e. Guangdong army.

92   i.e. the Guangxi army from the neighbouring province.

93   Meaning literally "south suburb" and "western suburb".

94   Other reports from the time say the gates were closed at 10pm nightly.

tung or Kwang-si, what difference? It is loot that they want."

With many "Hos" and "Hois" from the coolies we were carried down narrow stone steps – and back a thousand years. The native city of Canton, or Kwang-tung as the inhabitants call it, unrolled on either side like a fabulous scroll, the scroll of some ancient artist whose conception was too incredible to be real.

I was carried, careening and swaying, down alleys, past endless rows of shops and dwellings; strange ideographed signs, some painted on cloth and suspended overhead, others on wood or tin and hanging lengthwise beside open doorways. I was plunged into lanes where the air crawled with the odours of fish and fowl and swine (and who knows what else?); all displayed, and at the mercy of flies and other insects. I crossed viscid canals and wide gutters blue with scum... The intricacy of the streets; streets that twisted and curled, streets that ran straight and seemed to go on interminably; some boarded, some stone-flagged or paved, and others of uncovered dirt.

Canton, in retrospect, appears uncertain, illusory, a place seen through a cobweb. Behind this gauzy filament are faces, a multitude of yellow faces, all sombre, with the suffering of ages expressed in melancholy eyes and sharp, almost cruel features; swarms of faces that multiply until, in my confused imagination, they seem heaped together like piles of rusty coins. Now and then the cobweb is torn and I have a clear glimpse. A beggar, maimed and whining; a leper, his feet bound with cloth; an ancient wall, relic of the Ming dynasty; a shop where silks flash furtively from dark shelves, and large peacock fans makes suns of colour in the dusk…[95]

But for those shops Canton would be a duotone in grey and black. One comes upon them suddenly, buried in some impossible lane or facing a street foul with refuse. Great metal bars, set crosswise in a wooden frame, protect them from thieves. Within, displayed by importuning merchants, are foamy laces, and linens that have a sheer, poignant fragrance; ivory and precious stones; kingfisher work and sandalwood, and magnificent Spanish-Chinese shawls – heavy silk squares, weighted with fringe and embroidery and flaming with colour. I recall one in particular, a shawl purple as passion and embroidered in deep magenta. Had I bought it, as I was tempted to do, I know that, in America, it would have become a thing of brutal vividness, as ghastly as an exotic woman transplanted from her native luxury into a setting wholly commonplace. But there in Canton it was a brilliant gesture, a reflex of colour from that period when Ming and Spaniard moved against a background of opulent and barbaric.

---

95   The Ming Dynasty, 1368-1644.

On that first venture into the native city I went through a bewildering number of temples, not that I wished to visit so many in one afternoon (or at all, for that matter), but my guide considered it the thing to do. My protests did not so much as ripple his Confucian calm. Very solemnly, and with inherent dignity, he conducted me from temple to temple. The Kwang Hau Temple, the Temple of Longevity, the Flowery Forest Monastery, the Chun-ka-chie… Sepulchres all, haunted by ghosts of grandeur. The once marvellous carvings, now covered with dust and spider-webs, were crumbling to decay; the gold-leaf was tarnished and peeling. The very images, peering out from bat-guano and mouldy altar-ornaments, were eloquent of decadence.

Troops were quartered in some. The cloisters were being used as stables; the courtyards were buried in filth and dung. My guide said that the soldiers belonged to Dr. Sun's army. Young fellows they were, some less than sixteen, with a wishful hungering in their eyes. They wore drab grey uniforms, a colour so depressing, in that cheerless setting, that even the red bands on their caps could not lighten the effect. Boy soldiers, playing at war; attracted by the smell of gunpowder or inflamed by promises of plunder… One cannot soon forget the aching desolation of those Cantonese temples, their courts packed with mulch and offal, and peopled with slim boys waiting to die...

As a final touch of gloom, my guide took me to the City of the Dead, a series of buildings where, in the midst of white funeral banners and scarlet trappings, bodies were reposing to await a propitious day for burial. A place of flawless silence: candles on the altar, a musklike odour enriching the air. I wandered among alcoves containing coffins of ebony and sandalwood, followed by a solemn attendant who explained in detail the history of each corpse. There were three grades of service tendered the bodies, he said, the highest costing twenty dollars, the next ten dollars, and the lowest eight dollars... A distressing experience, this City of the Dead, not because of its purpose, but because of its significance. To me, it expressed with tragic eloquence the Chinese character – a mixture of superstition, obedience to custom, and infinite patience.

On the way back to the hotel a queer incident occurred. We were in a street so narrow that the people had to flatten themselves against the walls to let my sedan-chair pass. I happened to glance toward a doorway on my left just as a man appeared from the gloom within. He wore a long black Chinese coat and a skullcap. Indeed, he was dressed so inconspicuously that I might not have observed him beyond that one glance had he not paused at sight of me and stepped back. Then, with a suddenness that drove home like a physical shock, I saw that his eyes were blue, his skin white, and his features anything but Oriental... He vanished, lost in the dusk within, and I went rocking along the narrow, smelly street, aware that, for a moment, Romance had touched me.

Why was he, a white man in Chinese costume, there in the native city? I wondered; and I shall wonder always. A police officer? Too melodramatic. A criminal? Probable enough. A beachcomber, some wretched soul who simply wished to lose himself?[96] If so, I know of no place where he could do it with such ease. But, whatever he may have been, he was, to me Romance; and he gave Canton an added sense of tremendous and mysterious activity.

3.

After dinner my guide appeared with suggestions for the disposal of the evening. I could go to a restaurant in the old city and enjoy Chinese food and Chinese wine while a singsong girl entertained me by making falsetto

---

96   "Beachcomber" was a common term at the time along the China Coast for a white man living as a drifter or loafer with no particular occupation or source of income.

sounds and clapping to wooden blocks in my ear. Or, if I preferred, I could visit the Flower Boats.

The Flower Boats? I inquired.

Yes, where the prostitutes lived…

I dare say I looked mildly annoyed, for immediately he assured me that all the white gentlemen visited the Flower Boats if only for a "looksee."…

And so we took a sampan on the river. About us the darkness was ash-purple and sequined with lights. A warm stench rose from the water, heavy with the smell of sour mud and swill. Other sampans were gliding and scraping over mud-shallows: throaty ejaculations, fragments of song, came from the boatmen, and the muffled clash of cymbals sounded in some house on the bank. There was a certain beat and rhythm in the night, a heavy, measured throbbing, like that of a heart old and afflicted.

I remarked upon the unceasing activity, and my guide told me that more than a million creatures – I cannot call them human beings – live on the canals and the Chu-kiang.[97] They have strange customs, these river-dwellers, or *ta-min* as they are called, some of which I learned as we stole out silently toward the Flower Boats.[98] They are

---

97 The Zhujiang, known in English at the time more commonly as the Pearl, or Canton, River.

98 As regards "*ta-min*" I do not know this phrase, have never come across it before and cannot find any usages other than

89

social outcasts, and from among them come the *tan-ki-mui*, or singing-girls.[99] In their rules governing women there is the usual Eastern injustice: a wife is not allowed to leave the boat; there, in that small space, she eats, sleeps, works, and dies. But custom is more lenient with the man: he may have as many concubines as he can support; this luxury, however, may not be indulged until after he has acquired a legitimate wife called the *kit-fat*, or Number One Wife.[100]

"The Flower Boats," explained my guide, "apart from their ornate decorations, are distinguished from other house-boats by the letter 'D.'" And he added with subtle innuendo: "They are licensed, and the *loquiia* under medical observance."

We approached a copperish burst of light, and, after silent manoeuvring, scraped a platform. I could see by

---

Hervey's here.

99   Again I can find no other usage of the phrase *tan-ki-mui*, apart from Hervey's, though I assume he is referring to the waterborne Tanka people of Southern China.

100   *Kit-Fat*, meaning literally 'to tie up hair', refers to a first marriage between a spinster and a bachelor. She becomes the *kit-fat*. A woman who marries a widower becomes a *tin-fong* (meaning literally 'to fill a room'). I am grateful to Athena Nga Chee Liu's book, *Family Law in the Hong Kong SAR*, (Hong Kong: Hong Kong University Press, 1999) for this explanation.

the glow reflected from within that the front of the main structure was elaborately carved and gilded.

A fat, oily Chinaman met me on the deck and pushed me between silk curtains. Several little girls, vermillion-lipped and white-faced, greeted me as I entered. Evidently business was poor, for there were no masculine occupants.

I was conducted to a couch where I sat, quit stupidly I am sure, while those queer little courtesans, gathered in a semi-circle about me, giggled and made remarks that, had I understood them, would have been interesting if not elevating. The proprietor urged me to take my choice; the guide hovered in the doorway, registering disapproval of my conservatism.

I found something sharply pathetic about those tiny girls in brocaded jackets and satin trousers. I didn't pity them because of their profession, for I realized that they knew nothing better, nor was my reaction a sudden altruistic interest in their souls. I was thinking of their bodies; of the atmosphere in which they lived, the foul river air that fed their lungs, the lack of proper food and normal pleasure; the raw, drenching winters... The very fact of their existence seemed incredibly ironic and cruel. They were superfluous lives, the result of some profligate creative scheme; a scheme that had overcrowded Canton with millions of apparently purposeless bodies whose very presence in such a compact mass, was the cause of their extermination.

The proprietor looked disappointed when he learned that I was merely an observer. However, he succeeded in forcing some vitriolic rice-wine upon me, and bade one of the *loquiia* sing, in return for coins to be distributed among the courtesans. When I moved to depart, one little creature became quite excited, shrieking and clinging to my coat.

"She wishes to be kissed," my guide explained, solemnly.

…The emotional one followed us outside, and as we drifted away, she made a tiny silhouette against the silken curtains of the Flower Boat; to me, a gauze-winged creature caught and fluttering in a huge paper lantern.

"Tu-nai-amah!" she squealed, persistent to the last.

Which, my guide informed me voluntarily, had something to do with my grandmother and was decidedly unflattering.

4.

The name "Canton" invariably brings to my mind an incident pressed indelibly into the sheaves of boyhood memories. A cold, misty November dusk: the blue darkness sifting down outside, the pallid moon-fire of frost on the lawn; and, within, the humming fire and a man with a widow's peak who sat buried in an immense velour chair, talking of China. I was seven or eight at the time, and my knowledge of China was vague, coloured chiefly by dragons and a jade ring that my mother wore. But the country had a subtle fascination for me, and, dimly, I sensed that it was woven into my youth and manhood. And so I listened, hypnotized, as the man with the widow's peak told of his experiences in the far Flowery Kingdom. He talked mostly of a certain Doctor of Canton, one Sun Yat Sen, whose life was a succession of adventures and intrigues; of his plots against the Manchu throne, and his breathless escapes and flights... Immediately, and inevitably, the Doctor of Canton became, to me, the supreme expression of Adventure, a figure surrounded by dragons and jade rings. During the following years he lived magnificently in my imagination. Even after I was considerably older, he haunted my fancy...

Before I went to Canton I knew that the Doctor – now much more than a physician – lived there; and I determined to see him and talk with him. To this end, I obtained a letter of introduction in Hong-kong to a certain Chinese gentleman in Canton who was (and, I trust, still is) a close friend of Sun Yat Sen. Accordingly, one afternoon a day or so after my arrival, I set out in a sedan-chair for this gentleman's residence. It was some distance from Shameen, near the outskirts of the city, and when I arrived it was rather late. A fuchsia-red sun dipped behind mauve and sable roofs, leaving an orange stain on the sky. The walled house and surrounding country had that peculiar wild desolation that attends the sunset.

I was admitted into a garden unexpectedly charming and quaint as one of Pan Chih Yu's poems.[101] A pond lay half smothered in lotus-leaves, and butterfly-trees, their pink blossoms lithely astir, seemed to drench the dusk in pallid rain. By the water was a pygmy pavilion, eaves tilted impertinently toward the sky. I half expected to come upon some tiny maiden playing a moon-guitar.[102] I found, instead, a frail old lady who vanished quickly, tortuously on "golden-lily" feet; a grey moth put to flight by my intrusion.[103]

---

101 Pan Chih Yu lived in China in the first century BC. He was a noted wit and poet and a favourite at the imperial court. He has been referred to as the "Chinese Sappho". I expect the poem Hervey has in mind is *The Fan*, which was presented to the Emperor inscribed on a fan. See Appendix II.

102 Moon-guitar is another name for the Chinese traditional string instrument, the *yueqin* – a lute with a round, hollow wooden body (hence the nickname), a short fretted neck and four strings.

103 i.e. bound feet.

I waited, drunk with fancies, while a servant went to summon the master of the house. The air was saturated with silence, and high overhead, a wedge of birds was driven into the sky. The sudden peace of the place, the tranquil beauty of the pavilion, the walls and shrubs, all melting into the twilight, seemed to wound my imagination with a sense of poignant loveliness. I could see the garden in the past, with my maiden of the moon-guitar in the pavilion, and at her feet camphor-wood chests and silks, ivory and peacock feathers, brought by some lover from far Tartary or Tibet…[104]

And then a figure came through the dusk. My host looked important enough to wear the red button and peacock-feather of a high court official. Dark robes and a dark skullcap; a face that in the half-light, seemed moulded in porcelain.

He held my letter of introduction close to his eyes…

Would I honour him by coming inside?

Why not sit in the garden, I suggested, in the pavilion?

---

104 Tartary being a moveable feast of geographic indeterminism at the time and usually encompassing Central Asia from the Caspian Sea to the Urals and the Pacific and often also including Mongolia (outer and inner) as well as Manchuria.

He seemed pleased that I liked his garden, and sent a servant to brew tea.

We sat there by the green-black pool which, in the gloaming, became a shimmering incense-bowl that offered up sweet smoke to the dusk.

When polite formalities had been observed, I announced the purpose of my visit. I had been informed that he knew the Doctor of Canton well. I said, and I wondered if it would be possible for him to arrange a meeting.

He beamed. To serve me would be an honour.

But the Doctor was a busy man...

Oh, but he was always delighted to received foreign visitors, particularly Americans. Of course, there was some slight trouble at present... Kwang-tung and Kwang-si... But an interview could be arranged.

I told then of the man with the widow's peak and of my boyhood fancies.

He continued to beam. He spoke liquid syllables... A great man, Sun Wen (Sun Yat Sen's official name).[105] A noble man, and a true patriot. He was born between Canton and Macao; did I know that? Humble parents, but

---

105 Sun was born Sun Wen, while his genealogical name was Sun Deming. He was (and is still in mainland China) also known as Sun Zhongshan. Yat-sen was his pen name taken while living in Hong Kong.

very honourable. Sun's father was a Christian convert, and he saw to it that his son had the proper education. Sun was twenty when he entered the college of medicine at Macao. A brilliant student who became a brilliant surgeon but it was China's political troubles that challenged his genius. He threw his whole life into the cause of the people and determined to effect the overthrow of the Manchus…

The servant came with tea: fragrant Kee-choung…[106]

Sun travelled the length and breadth of China, often in disguise, risking torture and death, to preach his doctrine. (Thus my host between sips of tea). He demanded justice for the people, a free press, the proper educational facilities, and relief from the long oppression of the mandarins… He was a member of a secret organization in Canton of which there were eighteen members – and eventually seventeen were caught and beheaded. Sun always escaped. It was his personality. He drew men and dominated them. Persecuted, and with a price on his head, he continued to stir the multitudes. Once in Swatow there was a rebellion.[107] Sun and his followers persuaded the revolutionists to join forces with them in an attempt to capture Canton. When the time came, the Swatow troops were prevented from lending their aid through the treachery of one of their members, who

---

106   A high-class grade of Foochow (or Fuzhou) tea.

107   Now Shantou in Guangdong province.

informed the authorities of the planned uprising. Sun's small army was waiting at Hong-kong to sail up the river to Canton. A telegram was despatched from Swatow apprising the commanding officer of conditions there; but he misread the message, and the troops were sent to Canton – only to be captured in a body. The leaders, Sun among them, destroyed all papers in their headquarters in Canton and fled. Sun managed to work his way to Macao, where he was hidden by friends. But Macao became too dangerous for him. He went to Hong-kong… Kobe… Honolulu… San Francisco… London. The hand of the Manchu's reached far. There, in British territory, Sun was kidnapped and held prisoner in the Chinese legation for twelve days.[108] The British government, learning of his plight, forced his release…

But that was only one of his many exploits. During his travels in foreign lands he obtained great amounts of money from native sons of Han living abroad, and bought arms and ammunition which were smuggled into China… The great day came: a Manchu edict declared the Celestial Empire a republic. Sun, in London at the time, was asked to be President. But he was a modest man (he who had brought about the downfall of the Manchus),

---

108   The Chinese Embassy building on Portland Place, W1.

and he declined, stating that Yuan Shi-k'ai would be a more executive than he.[109]

Thus, briefly, the story of the Doctor of Canton.

Darkness has thickened, and the garden was mottled with shadows of violet and grey. Pearls were in the incense-bowl: a few reflected stars caught in the still black water. My host was lithely rubbing his hands: night had lined the air with a raw chill.

I rose. He would go inside and write a note to Sun Wen, he announced. Would I not come in, too? The night air…

Afterward he accompanied me to the gate. As I turned for a last look at the garden, I saw a shadow form by the pool. Perhaps it was a maid with sloe-dark eyes, playing a moon-guitar.

5.

I awoke to the sombre opulence of another day – I say sombre for even the hazed sun which had slipped through the clouds could not destroy the melancholy of Canton – and, after breakfast, despatched the letter to Sun Yat Sen.

I shall be delighted to see you this afternoon –

109   See footnote 46.

And so I went to meet the Doctor of Canton…

A sampan, curtained and painted red, took me across the river, past a scarred Chinese warship anchored in midstream and the wharf of the headquarters of South China. a guard of grey-clad soldiers were waiting, their uniforms extraordinarily clean. Pale sunshine ran a tongue of light along their bayonets. With the rattle of accoutrements, the clack of heels on stone, I was escorted past more guards, through a yellowed courtyard and into the cellar-like gloom of a hall. Stairs ascended into a rectangle of light, and up we went. At the top my credentials were examined for the second time, the guard dismissed, and I followed a smiling secretary into a room that, obviously, was the meeting-place of the cabinet. A long table, green-topped, and rows of chairs; bare floor and bare walls. The secretary disappeared; I was alone.

As I waited, wrapped about with silence, I felt a thrilling intimacy with intrigue. It was a setting of melodrama: the long cabinet room, the leaden sky heavy with swollen clouds, and the scarred war-ship in midstream awaiting any emergency.

Suddenly a man in khaki moved out quietly from behind a screen in the far end. He advanced toward me, smiling, a gleam in his friendly eyes, and I realized that he was the Doctor of Canton.

We shook hands and sat down; I with veins of excitement spraying my spine.

"You have come at an unpleasant time," he began, in a cultured, genial voice.

His enunciation was perfect. But that was not surprising, as he is a college graduate. What did surprise me was that this gracious, mild-mannered Chinese was the romantic figure of my boyhood fancies, the man who had knocked the rotted foundations from under the Manchu dynasty; who had refused the presidency of the young republic, but, later, when his country was threatened with disintegration, had declared himself President of the South in defiance of the corrupt Northern Government.[110]

"The customs affair has upset us considerably," he said, "and upset us mentally more than politically. It shows what South China might expect from the powers – particularly America." He paused; looked grave. "I regret very much the action of your Government in sending war-ships to Canton."

He referred to the then recent seizure of the customs fund by his party and the swift action of the European and American powers in dispatching a fleet of gunboats to Canton.

---

110   i.e. the government then in Beijing, also known as the Beiyang government.

"We of South China did look to America for friendship – and recognition," he went on. "The United States, if we could only make her see it, can mould China into a great republic like herself." He nodded; I remember that vividly, for it seemed to italicize his statement. "The Peking Powers have not made for a united republic; in fact, under Tsao Kun, they are daily getting father away from it.[111] We of the South have the means of progress of we only had the power. That power is recognition of our Government, which, of course, means credit. With credit we could virtually do the rest alone."

Although physically he was not as I had visualized him, his personality blended with his adventurous history; a sheer, commanding personality. His words were carefully chosen, were placed with the exquisite precision of mosaic-work. As he talked, I was back in the fire-lit room of my boyhood, while the blue dusk sifting down and the hoar-frost on the lawn.

"I have a plan which I call the International Development Scheme," he continued. "Co-operation, not fighting, is my principle. But" – and his eyes took on a fierce gleam – "if necessary, I will fight to attain the ultimate peace that means co-operation. International war, commercial war, and class war; those are the three great conflicts in China. International war, as we know,

111   China's sixth president and in-situ during Hervey's stay.

is simply organized brigandage on a tremendous scale; a terrible thing. When America entered the European War she did so to put an end to all wars. We had great hope, we of China, believing that what we call *Tatung*, or the Age of Great Harmony, was about to begin. But, although successful in war, America failed in peace. The world has been thrown back into chaotic conditions. Greed and lust have gripped Europe again; she needs materials for new wars to come... And China would be a valuable acquisition. China, after hundreds of years of slumber, is waking, realizing that she must obey the mandate of progress. She can organize for peace or for war. With the menace of Europe and Japan over her, how does she dare to think of peace? The militarists of the North wish to Prussianize China; I desire to have her cemented into a republic so powerful in her peace that other nations will be afraid to molest her. To do this, we must organize from within. And I am wondering if it can be done with the pen or with the sword."

The sun had gone; rain fell in a fine sifting of grey ash. But the dampness could not chill me. The optimism of the man flowed through me in subtle warmth. It no longer seemed incongruous that this was he who, failing in his first attempt to overthrow Yehonala, the Manchu woman, had escaped and fled from Canton to Macao, and thence by devious ways to America and England, enlisting sympathy and aid as he travelled, until, his support strengthened morally and materially, he had returned to make actual his dream of a republic. I was, suddenly, hopeful in the face of towering difficulties. I could see China, the mighty dragon, crawling from her bed of ancient corruption, to a place in the sun.

"It might be done with the pen," he resumed, "if the powers would keep out. But, as we have seen, they will not. Very well. China is waking, I said. If the powers will not relinquish their grasp peacefully, China will see what the pressure of her millions of population, organized into a great army, can do to persuade them."

Again his eyes flashed. Behind him, through an open window, I could see the war-ship anchored in midstream; a reminder that at any moment he might be forced to seek the protection of its grey gun-turrets... And yet he dared to dream of a militant China carrying his ideals into actual physical struggle with the world!

"I spoke of a plan for international development," he said. "A phase of this scheme is to make possible a greater usage of our national resources. Regulate the Yang-tse, improve the railway systems, construct ports, and improve our clothing and food industries. These tings must be done. For instance, I have plans for the development of Canton into a world port. With the establishment of shipyards, a good railway, proper docking facilities, and an improvement of its waterway, it will be not only the largest city in China, but the greatest port. Its advance as a commercial centre will not injure Hong-kong as a free port; it will simply make competition keener. And competition is the main structure of development. Of course, you say this will take years. Perhaps. Canton, I admit, is in a state of chaos. But it is a revolutionary city. When fighting ceases it will become normal. At present we have no finances. We have nothing more tangible than our dreams…"

Sun Yat Sen closed his narrow eyes thoughtfully.

Except for the soft rain and he creaking of floors in the hall where grey-capped guards moved, there was an uncanny stillness. Suddenly, the little man looked up.

"One common language and one common coin," he announced. "They alone can bring about the national unity that is so vital to the preservation of China."

"But isn't that impossible?" I suggested. "At least, in this generation?"

"Impossible? Yes – as long as the Powers hold China a slave to their interests. If the money of Hong-kong and Canton were the same, the international banks would lose a valuable percentage of exchange. And if the people of the various provinces spoke the same tongue there would be less cause for internal strife – which would be fatal to foreign interests."

He talked on, the footsteps of the sentries punctuating his remarks. I do not remember all that he said; his personality submerged words. But I can recall that I felt as though a soft filament was being woven before my eyes, a cobweb of dreams. Splendid dreams, and so fragile that they seemed incapable of holding the monster China in their gossamer bonds.

When I left, the rain was falling harder. It flung a chilling dampness upon the ardour that Sun had aroused. "Nothing more tangible than dreams…" On the far shore, a column of troops were marching away from their barracks, many of them, I fancied, sombre-faced boys, like those in her dung-littered temples. They brought to mind the profligate mass of decadent life that crawled and swarmed through the intricate streets and on the canals; the City of the Dead; the Flower Boats; the temples with their tarnished gold-leaf and rotting splendours. "Nothing more tangible than dreams." Dreams! Dreams stirring like ghosts among ruins… dreams…

And, suddenly, it seemed that I was in a vast City of the Dead, and that China, old China, was a corpse awaiting a propitious day for burial.

APPENDIX I

The Green Tea Land
One Piece Sing-Song Californee-Side

> *Wat-tim he almon' flower hab white when peach-tlee blongey[112] pink,*
> *My smokey opium-pipe, galaw[113], an' munchee tim' my tink*
> *'Bout all pidgin China-side no fan-kwei[114] understand,*
> *In olo Fei-Chaw-Shang[115] inside – my nicee Gleen-Tea Land.*
>
> *Some tim my make dleam-pidgin an' lidee on he wind*
> *Acloss he yaong (the ocean) to allo my leave 'hind,*

---

112   To have, or a characteristic belonging to.

113   A word without meaning, an interjection.

114   *Fan-kwei* (sometimes *fanqui*) meaning 'foreign devils' – i.e. Europeans and Americans.

115   An alternative name for Canton (Guangzhou).

Where willow-tlee – all same golo[116] in sun go-down-shine stand,
In olo Fei-Chaw-Shang inside – my nicee Gleen-Tea Land.

My hearee one tim China-side flom velly olo witch,
Supposey my go fan-kwei land, my getee plenty lich.
What-tim my catchee pay dirt now, an' cash come plenty hand,
My wailo[117] hom to Fei-Chaw-Shang – my olo Gleen-Tea Land.

T'here bottom-side he shiney moon at housee I look-see,
An' fishee 'mong he lo flower long-side he lunyantlee;
Supposey die, my catchee glave where wise man command,
All plopa China-fashion in he nicey Gleen-Tea Land.

Contained within Charles G Leland, *Pidgin-English Sing-Song or Songs and Stories in the China-English Dialect* (London: Trübner & Co., 1876), p.63-64.

---

116   Gold.
117   To depart, to go away.

APPENDIX II

The Fan by Pan Chih Yu

Of fresh new silk, all snowy white,
And round as harvest moon;
A pledge of purity and love,
A small but welcome boon.

While summer lasts, borne in the hand
Or folded on thy breast,
'Twill gently soothe thy burning brow,
and charm thee to thy rest.

But ah! When autumn frosts descend,
And winter's winds blow cold,
No longer sought, no longer loved,
'Twill lie in dust and mould.

This silken fan, then deign accept,
Sad emblem of my lot –
Caressed and fondled for an hour,
Then speedily forgot.

APPENDIX III

Christopher J Murphy Jr.

Hervey was good friends with the artist Christopher Murphy (Jr.), though it's not entirely clear whether or not they ever travelled to China and Asia together. Murphy provided the illustrations that accompany Hervey's travelogue of the Far East, *Where Strange Gods Call: Pages Out of the East*, though these are, most probably, adaptations from postcards or photographs. Similarly, although Hervey does not mention a travelling companion in the book it is possible he was travelling with Murphy as he later travelled with Carleton Hildreth.

Certainly, Hervey and Murphy were friends and contemporaries. They were born within two years of each other – Hervey in 1900; Murphy in 1902 – and both had attended military schools and spent time in Savannah, Georgia. Christopher Aristide Desbouillons Murphy was born in Savannah to an artistic family. He was the eldest of seven children, the son of Christopher Patrick Hussey Murphy (1869-1939) and Lucile Desbouillons Murphy (1873-1956), who were both recognized local artists.

Murphy Jr. began formal lessons at a young age and later at the Art Students League in New York in 1921. His paintings were shown in New York and back home at the 1924 Southern Art League exhibition in Telfair, Georgia. Murphy received the prestigious Louis Comfort Tiffany Foundation Fellowship in 1925, and once again exhibited in the Southern Art League's annual exhibition at the Atlanta Biltmore Hotel. *The Atlanta Constitution* noted, 'Christopher Murphy Jr., of Savannah, is a coming portrait painter if his "Portrait of Miss M." be a prophecy. It is one thing to get form and color and another thing to catch a personality.'[118] Between 1925 and 1930 Murphy divided his time between Savannah and New York continuing to study and also working as a commercial artist. He was considered particularly expert in etching though also worked in watercolour, gouache, etching and dry paint and oil.

It seems Murphy Jr. and Hervey had first encountered each other in 1923 in Savannah perhaps when Hervey was giving public lectures with titles such as "Kipling and India, Conrad and the South Seas and Pierre Loti and Franco-Indo China".[119] Hervey's biographer, Harlan

118 'Entire South Represented in Southern Art League Exhibit', *The Atlanta Constitution*, April 16, 1925, p.15.
119 Harlan Greene, *The Damned Don't Cry – They Just Disappear: The Life and Works of Harry Hervey* (Columbia,

Greene, believes Hervey convinced Murphy Jr. to provide the pen and ink drawings that accompany *Where Strange Gods Call*. Greene indicates that Murphy Jr. had not himself travelled to Asia and that we can only guess how he was able to replicate scenes from the region. Greene suggests that, 'Most likely his [Murphy Jr.'s] illustrations were drafted from photographs Hervey had taken. Many of Murphy's illustrations do, in fact, have that snapshot quality, while others have the staged appearance of post cards.'[120] This does indeed seem the best educated guess. Of the five illustrations Murphy Jr. provided of Macao and Canton (no illustrations of Hong Kong are included) most are common scenes from postcards popular with visiting Europeans and Americans (the Canton waterfront, street scene and the notorious "flower boats" as well as the Macao scene).

Murphy Jr. and Hervey were to collaborate again in his career – Murphy Jr. painted a portrait of Hervey to accompany a newspaper article in 1925 and also provided a cover illustration for Hervey's 1928 novel set in French

---

South Carolina: University of South Carolina Press, 2018), p.35.

120   Ibid, p.40. Sadly it seems none of the original photographs or postcards have survived.

Indo-China, *Congaï: Mistress of Indochine.*[121] However, the vast bulk of Murphy Jr.'s work was concerned with portraying the American South. A 1928 review of his exhibition of seventy-five etchings and pencil drawings held at the Plainfield (New Jersey) Library Art Gallery noted that the majority of the subjects were, '…country places, interesting architecture, sketches of gateways, church towers, water fonts and Negro cabins near the rice fields, all of which are worth owning as valuable bits of Americana.'[122]

Murphy Jr. remained based in Savannah and married Ernestine Cole in 1946. They had one son, Christopher Cole Murphy. Christopher Murphy Jr. died in 1973.

121   Harry Hervey, *Congaï: Mistress of Indochine* (London: Thornton Butterworth, 1928).
122   'Etching Exhibit to Close Sunday', *The Courier-News* (Bridgewater, New Jersey), April 13, 1928, p.31.

ACKNOWLEDGEMENTS

My thanks to Megan Walsh Gerard who found time to visit the Georgia Historical Society Archives in Savannah to search for Harry Hervey's movie treatments and Asian-set short stories. Also, Hervey's principal biographer Harlan Greene, who kindly encouraged further explorations of Harry's Asian sojourns. Jonathan Wattis of Wattis Fine Art in Hong Kong kindly provided some additional details of Christopher J Murphy's life and work. The librarians and archivists at the Georgia Historical Society Archives kindly answered my queries and promptly sent documents to me. The London Library holds the copy of the British first edition of Hervey's *Where Strange Gods Call: Pages Out of the East* that I consulted for this text. Michael Duckworth, who in a past life was my supportive publisher at the Hong Kong University Press, offered some help with manuscripts and sources. Dr Anne Witchard read and edited the notes and appendices with her usual sharp eye.